Sell What You Grow

Other Books By Mimi Luebbermann

Beautiful Bulbs
Bread Baking with Herbs
Cactus and Succulent Gardens
Climbing Vines
Easy Orchids
Heirloom Gardens
Homegrown Fruit
Little Herb Gardens
Little Potted Gardens
Miscarriage Grief
Salad Gardens
Shade Gardens
Terrific Tomatoes
Vegetables Gardens
The Williams-Sonoma Wedding Planner

Sell What You Grow

How to Take Your Herbs and Produce to Market for Serious Cash

Mimi Luebbermann

PRIMA PUBLISHING
3000 Lava Ridge Court ■ Roseville, California 95661
(800) 632-8676 ■ www.primalifestyles.com

PRIMA PUBLISHING and colophon are trademarks of Prima Communications Inc., registered with the United States Patent and Trademark Office.
Previously published by Prima under the title Pay Dirt.

Library of Congress Cataloging-in-Publication Data
Luebbermann, Mimi
    Sell what you grow : how to take your herbs and produce to market for serious cash/Mimi Luebbermann.
        p. cm.
    Includes bibliographical references and index.
    ISBN 0-7615-2299-9
1. Herb gardening. 2. Herbs—Marketing.
3. Vegetables—Marketing.
I. Title.
SB351.H5L85 1997
635'.7'0688—dc21   96-49878
                                                      CIP

00 01 02 03 04 AA 10 9 8 7 6 5 4 3 2 1

Printed in the United States of America

How to Order
Single copies may be ordered from Prima Publishing, 3000 Lava Ridge Court, Roseville, CA 95661; telephone (800) 632-8676. Quantity discounts are also available. On your letterhead, include information concerning the intended use of the books and the number of books you wish to purchase.

Visit us online at www.primalifestyles.com

In memory of
Gene Reed Prendergast
and Joseph Prendergast,
Oak Hill Farm, Virginia

CONTENTS

Preface ix

Acknowledgments xv

1 Digging Right In 1
2 The Pros and Cons of Organic
   Farming 11
3 Growing Specialty Vegetables
   and Herbs 25
4 Treasures: Foraging
   for Profit 42
5 Selling a Value-Added
   Product 57
6 From the Farm to the Table:
   Selling Your Products 74
7 Country to City
   Connections 101
8 Great Ideas for City
   Gardeners 119
9 Bureaucratic Hurdles 132
10 Paying the Mortgage: Success
   Stories from Around
   America 144
11 Old-Fashioned Farm Thrift 171
12 Obtaining Helpful Sources
   through the Internet 191

Afterword   197
A Compendium of Wild and Useful Ideas   199
Crop Production Bibliography   207
Seed Sources   209
Bulb Sources   213
Professional Associations   217
Sources of Printed Materials on Small-Scale
    Farming   219
Index   221

PREFACE

I was a nonpracticing farmer when I wrote the first edition of *Pay Dirt*. At that time, I had created a professional niche working for farm groups with specialty products so I could, even though living in the city, at least rub shoulders with farming, farm practices, and farmers. Conferences, farm visits, and seminars helped me learn about the resources available to farmers, as well as the issues involved, and I came to appreciate the difficulties entailed in running a profitable farm. At the time, I was confident I had a firm grasp on the important concepts of farming and marketing specialty products from my interviews and on-site experiences, but at the same time, I had a prickling, uncomfortable feeling that I wasn't out there hoeing, mowing, pickling, or selling on a "need-to-make-a-living-farming" basis.

I know now that there lurked a deeper motive for my interest in farming; I really wanted to move back to the farm myself. My family had left a farm in Virginia when I was seven years old, too early for much agricultural education or, more to the point, farm chores. I remember crying as we drove for the last time down the long driveway, squirming around in my seat to get the very last sight of the old white farmhouse with green shutters, crossing over the bridge at the creek, past the lake, and turning onto the road, with a last glimpse flashing by of the house surrounded by oak trees.

All my life I kept in touch with farming. At first I thought I was just interested in remembering my early youth, but a pattern began to emerge of going to fairs and visiting the animal buildings, watching James Herriot's television show about vetting in England, and enthusiastically gardening. Those brief early years I lived on the farm left me with the unforgettable scent of new-mown hay and recollections of puppies in the barn eating out of a piglet trough, baby chicks scurrying after their mother, and downy yellow ducklings floating in soft puffs on the lake. Farmers will chuckle reading this, noting there is no mention of trickling sweat from mucking out barns, torn hands from mending fences, the drip of leaking faucets, too-quiet pumps (they often stop in the middle of the night), or the cold fingers of an icy wet winter dawn spent with animals, hungry every day whether it rains or the sun shines.

Slowly, the conviction came to me that I wanted to move back to a farm, in fact, it seemed to me that I had to move back. I collected the Department of Agriculture books I remembered from my father's library, went to sheepdog trials at the state fair, and shyly admitted to people that I hoped one day, to be a farmer myself. I had lived most of my life in the city, but even there I kept rabbits and chickens, planted fruit trees, vegetables, and herbs, and canned year after year, traipsing out to greenbelt farms to bring back harvest-fresh fruits and vegetables. Neighbors complained about the cackling hens, but I gave them eggs. My sons harvested giant sunflowers and crisp golden delicious apples that they sold to the local produce store. Still, when I first moved into my farm in 1995, (twenty-five acres of grazing land in the Chileno Valley of Petaluma, California) I was not prepared.

I was not ready for gates that seemed to leave themselves open so the sheep wandered out on the road, for fences that fell over in the night, for tree limbs that blocked driveways, for the pitiful sight of a sick sheep standing, head down, alone under a tree, or the anxious gaze of a mother sheep when one of her babies lay still and dead on the floor of the lambing pen. I have learned to budget for vet bills, to give injections, and to negotiate with my sheep by food bucket so they do anything I ask, well, almost anything. Still, I wasn't ready for four partly eaten, prime laying hens and a bandit-faced raccoon, caught in the pen gazing at me stoically, unmoved by my wrath. With the help of a neighbor, I buried him soon after—farming priorities change your urban-formed priorities about wildlife preservation.

I wasn't ready for a mountain of fine-quality fleece that no one wanted to buy because its coarse fibers were only preferred by weavers, and the local weavers had bought during the spring or had their sources well established already. Having stood all day in ninety-plus degree heat at a spinning event, confident that I would go home with an empty truck—my fleeces were so beautiful—I wanted to give up when almost no one even came over to see my wool. I reloaded the truck with gritted teeth and sweaty brow. Then how was I to sell the eight ram lambs to save me the cost of butchering all of them? So much to learn, so little time, and no money to spare.

I wasn't ready for a tree laden with persimmons that had to be harvested hurriedly before the razor-billed blue jays drilled holes in all of them. I was, and still am, totally unprepared for a drive-way underneath the black walnut trees paved with the black walnuts. All this fruitfulness and no buyers; what was I to do?

So, speaking from experience, I have learned how much easier it is to advise someone else to do it than to do it myself. Farming teaches discipline,

time-clock regularity, and attention to detail. On-
the-job learning is stressful, anxiety producing,
and hard work; because when you get your job
done, you usually see how it could be done better,
so you start all over again. I will never forget the
kindness of a consoling pat from my veterinarian,
after two weeks of lambing, "You've had a tough
time haven't you?" he said, and he knew, because
I talked to him at least twice a day as each new
crisis occurred, from prolapses and induced
births, to a mother who cheerfully ate her baby's
tail just moments after it was born.

Just a note to mention one of my real trepida-
tions: the fear that my neighbors and community
would be inhospitable to a single woman, fifty
plus, and a city escapee, running a farm. I have
found quite the opposite; nothing but friendly
encouragement, advice and help (if solicited),
and a community welcome. Men understand well
the contributions of women to the partnership of
farming. Farm women drive tractors, run sheep,
manage huge dairies, fence, build, and do whatever is needed to make the farm run efficiently
and profitably. These men have seen that their
partners must have the skills to face any farm
emergency, because pipes burst, well pumps stop,
and cows go through fences or have their calves
without any warning, every farmer must know
what to do. If any single woman out there has a
dream of farming, fulfill it. Your community of
farm neighbors will assist you if you approach
them in a friendly fashion and ask openly for help
while offering your own in exchange. Typing for
fencing, jams for trenching, cups of coffee and
chat are basis of exchange and barter well-known
and still appreciated in the country.

Now, several years into the real world of farming,

I know that planting, harvesting, marketing, income and expenses, time, and weather fit together with a complexity and heartlessness that often approaches brutality. The fifteenth of every month, rain or snow (too early or too late), machines that break down just in the middle of a task, or animals that die come with a certitude that cannot be denied. Yet, those of us who watch the hills brighten with pink in the morning, listen to the first bleats between a glistening-wet, seconds-old lamb and its mother, watch the first lettuces spring up to cover beds with a blanket of green, or prop up limbs of trees that bow with fruit, don't think of giving up. If we do, we discard it quickly, sure that tomorrow will bring new solutions. The beauty that surrounds us, the neighborliness of our community, the white wave of a deer's tail, and the effortless flight of the hawk convince us we have chosen the right path. We make our way with simplistic optimistic determination—I will sell all my wool one year soon—and the delight in the exquisite pleasure of independence flavored by the light touch of the early morning breeze on our forehead. Farming is work, and work means bone-tired muscles, but it is real work; so we see the results, we taste the products, and we truly reap what we sow. For those of us with a calling to farm, love of animals and nature, and the pride and pleasure of dirt under our fingernails, we have no choice; we farm.

ACKNOWLEDGMENTS

Thanks to Martha Casselman, literary agent, who has the special gift to be both a friend and a business associate. And thanks to Jennifer Basye, the clipper who provided the idea for this book as well as encouragment and support in its development. To Andi Reese Brady, for editorial considerations, Anne Montague for copyediting, and Janelle Rohr and Bookman Productions, all of them essential in creating a book from a manuscript.

To my children, Arann and Daniel Harris—may they inherit a love for the land.

To Carolyn Miller, a friend and adviser whose skilled editorial talent matches only her bountiful encouragement of other writers.

Grateful appreciation for the help of the Small Farm Center, University of California, Davis, and to the corps of cooperative extension farm advisers. They have not only aided and encouraged my efforts, but they offer invaluable assistance to farmers all across America.

Thanks to those on farms, in forestry offices, in nurseries, and at conferences who have answered endless questions and shared their life experiences.

To the Organic Farming Research Foundation for its outstanding contribution to making our foods wholesome, and to the California Association of Family Farmers, who cajole, support, and network for the benefit of family farmers.

Finally, this book is dedicated to all those who work the land and pass on the rewards of stewardship, whether they own a handkerchief-size plot, work a community garden, or look to the horizon for their boundaries.

Sell What You Grow

CHAPTER 1

Digging Right In

There is a revolution going on all over America. Like many revolutions, it started quietly and then began to spread without much notice until suddenly you could not miss it. Across the country, market stands are bursting with the freshest skinny green beans, *mesclun* mixes of ten different lettuce varieties, neon-orange winter squash, blue mushrooms, pale endive, and overflowing baskets of apples, sometimes seven or eight varieties at a single stall. Farmers' markets introduce bright country swirls of color into the midst of gray cities, and basket-laden shoppers swap recipes with growers over pyramids of fingerling potatoes or rainbow-colored eggs of green, blue, pink, and speckled brown.

Articles in the *New York Times* and the *Wall Street Journal* describe city people selling lettuce grown in their backyards, loggers in Oregon switching from felling trees to raising herbs, and rural farmers making a go of it selling exotic birds and entertaining bed and breakfast guests in between harvesting blueberries. At the same time, in labored and earnest prose, these newspapers describe the death of the American farm. How can you tell what is really going on?

Farmers *are* battered by the global economy, by the flood of fruits and vegetables from abroad, the high price of land for beginning farmers, labor costs, expensive inputs of fertilizer, pesticides, and farm equipment. Besides these monumental problems, there are regulations that govern what boxes to ship produce in, size requirements for wholesale produce, complex taxes for farm employees both long term and casual, insurance companies worried about liability, and agricultural commissioner charges for farm inspections.

When the clatter of the headlines dies away, the simple truth emerges that regardless of the difficulties, more people than ever are turning to farming. Many who are farming intensively on small spaces are not included in the census-takers' statistics.

American farming has the reputation of being large, corporate, and run by business decisions, not culinary ideals. Yet when we recall the farms of America's past, we usually think of a simple rural scene with clapboard houses, rows of corn, and horses grazing. In a remarkable way, today's most successful small farmers are going back to the methods and philosophy of our forebears.

Originally, farmers came to America from all over the world to find land to support their families. This sustenance farming continued until people began to cluster in the cities. Eighteenth- and nineteenth-century city dwellers depended on farmers living on the outskirts to bring in food to be sold on the streets and in the markets. Once trains began to traverse the American plains, things began to change. Western cattle drives brought huge herds to the trains that delivered them to the stockyards of Chicago and the Midwest. The trains also brought oranges, nuts, and grains from California to the East, signaling the beginning of the end for diversified regional agriculture. The refrigerated boxcar, which came into use just before World War II, and airplanes created the luxury of eating food produced all over the nation and the world at any time of the year and enforced a trend toward bigger farms—plant plants, owned by companies with directors who had never sat on a tractor or dug up the soil.

In the early sixties, produce, from a small-farm outlook, was in a pretty deplorable state. Varieties of fruits and vegetables were developed and grown only for their ability to last from field to shelf. Many of the most delicious varieties were dropped because they were not able to travel across the country and arrive at the market in an edible condition. Fresh food was dried, pulverized, and instantized for the convenience of a nation in a hurry and enamored of food grown and made for them by other people. McDonald's (not Farmer MacDonald) served out millions of leathery hamburgers with a thin sliver of tomato and an anemic lettuce leaf. Salad in those days was a wedge of iceberg with Thousand Island dressing. Some older people who had grown up on farms spoke wistfully of tomatoes that tasted sweet; city people expected produce like that only when they returned to visit family back on the farm.

Those twenty years when prepared food seemed glamorous were followed by an educated disillusionment that continues to deepen today. Like a lot of things that glitter, the surface appearance of perfectly beautiful fruit wasn't matched by its substance, its taste and texture. People discovered that the flawless apple stored for six months had a mealy texture and minimal flavor, and they began to want real food again. Iceberg lettuce, delicious in its own way, was boring without other choices for different kinds of salad. Instant mashed potatoes paled in comparison to fresh potatoes just out of the garden, cooked and whipped to a snowy perfection.

Home cooks renewed their interest in preparing food, and Julia Child arrived on television with sophisticated techniques and encouragement.

In the early seventies, Alice Waters returned from France to Berkeley, California, and began to cook dinners with her friends. They enthusiastically encouraged her to open a small restaurant, which she proceeded to do, the now legendary Chez Panisse. She bought from grocery stores in the beginning, but she was disappointed with the results. Her friends brought their backyard lettuce in to the kitchen. Someone offered sorrel from her yard, and rabbits came from a hobbyist in Oakland, who exchanged the rabbits for dinners. Alice Waters orchestrated a production system of farmers, relatives, backyard growers, and amateurs to come up with fresh fruits and vegetables whose quality matched that of bygone years. Later, she worked with Sibella Kraus and a host of others to create a market for first-rate produce, rewarding quality with purchase. Small farmers in Northern California began to take heart, and they began to grow the very best products they could. Other restaurants got interested, in many cases because they were owned by chefs who had worked with Alice. Like ripples in a pond, the quest for quality products spread throughout California, and then throughout America. Restaurants, wholesalers, grocery stores, and specialty stores all sought to locate the finest fresh fruits and vegetables.

Anyone over thirty years old has witnessed the change in American food, but many people do not realize that we have really gone back to an efficient and effective system of farming started during the late 1800s. We have returned to old-fashioned market gardening, the tradition of small farms that encircle the city and bring fresh products daily to the consumer.

There are two notions in play that make this all work for the producer. The first is regional farming, which means that the food you eat was harvested as little as forty-eight hours before and within a hundred miles, instead of several weeks and over a thousand miles. The second is seasonal eating, enjoying the fruits and vegetables fresh from the earth, not from the storage sheds. To accomplish seasonal eating, consumers need to understand what is in season, difficult when they have never themselves harvested blueberries, and so may not realize that blueberries available in February are not grown in America.

Small family farms, long described in the media as a vanishing species, are actually making a comeback as the new-fangled small, highly efficient market farm that devotes itself to satisfying the modern appetite for fruits and vegetables with superb taste and texture. They bring to market produce and quality products that have been absent from grocery shelves for thirty or more years, as well as heirloom varieties, European specialties, and the finest offspring of the hybridizers.

These family farms might be small city backyards that supply a chef with arugula, or fifteen acres on the outskirts of a suburban community. Whatever their size or their products, they are changing the buying habits of consumers long resigned to frozen or plastic-wrapped produce.

Shoppers are heading to farmers' markets, where they can select fruits and vegetables picked dew-fresh. New York City has its Green Markets, Seattle has its Pike Street Market, Cincinnati has its century-old Findlay Market. Across America, city buyers make weekend excursions to small roadside stands in the sweet-smelling country. These urban-ites are hungry for the taste of real food, nourishing, delicious, and harvested at the height of freshness from the neighboring fields. Meeting the farmer who grows the sweet tomatoes, and inhaling the freshness of the crop, brings a pleasure to eating that the shopper pushing a cart down supermarket aisles will never know.

This book is designed for urban gardeners with large backyards, suburbanites living on larger greenswards, and farmers on the edge of cities. Re-tirees who move to the country, breadwinners working at full-time jobs, teachers with long summer vacations, and young families are turning to part-time farming for profit as well as personal satisfaction. There are a number of reasons that a variety of people from all walks of life are returning to farming. A kind of primal hunger for the work of the soil, a dissatisfaction with city culture, a desire to engage the whole family in a joint enterprise—all are driving men and women to try their hand at a lifestyle reminiscent of our ancestors'. Whether you live in the city with a couple of Golden Delicious apple trees in your backyard, or you have five acres and consider sheep automatic lawnmowers, there are ways you can turn situations into profit as large or as small, as demanding or as leisurely, as you want.

Besides raising real food, the creative new farmer can develop attractive products for bringing the outdoors into the urban environment, softening its hard concrete edges. An herbal wreath with a sub-tle fragrance of meadows and woods, for example, helps to offset the tensions of city life.

These sidelines are a part of the new market farmers' development as a redesigned economic unit. The trend toward bigger and bigger farms that began after World War II was accompanied by the urbanization that has laid the groundwork for today's burgeoning small-farm movement. Farms in greenbelts around cities supply small specialty produce stores, bring eggs, apples, fresh herbs, and lettuces to discriminating diners, and natural materials to florists and craft shops. The small nineteenth-century market gardeners used intensive gardening methods and were stingily economical in their farming techniques, producing crops all year round. Similarly, today's new farmers work to diversify their crop base, trying unusual potatoes for early spring, planting fruit trees in the manner of grapevines, and supplementing chicken feed with weeds and restaurant vegetable trimmings.

To succeed as a businessperson in a very competitive market, today's new farmer must assess the opportunities of the land, research specialty products, weigh the possibilities of the market, plan the crop, grow it, and then sell it.

Both new and established farmers determine their farm practices from an ecological and economical standpoint. Many farmers decide to farm without commercial chemicals as a personal and ethical statement; like all decisions, this one sets in motion a variety of effects which will determine the farm's profitability. To be sure, the market is starting to accept the higher prices of organic produce and herbs, and more processors, from Gerbers to Newman's Own, are buying organic products. There are drawbacks, however, which each farmer must also weigh and measure carefully. The regulatory agencies that certify farms as organic may require expensive renovations or processing procedures. Local markets may not wish to carry the more perishable organic produce, and chefs may not be willing to pay a premium for it when their customers do not seem to care. Chapter 2 discusses organic farming in detail. The most important part of growing vegetables and herbs is making informed decisions about top selling varieties suited to your climate, soil, land, and customers. Chapter 3 helps you understand the choices involved in selecting crops you can sell for a premium and the most efficient methods to grow them.

Regardless of the decision about what farm practices to follow, the farmer must become a savvy entrepreneur who looks to style magazines for the newest decorating and food trends, who strolls the farm to spot recycling opportunities that will allow prunings, weeds, or hedgerows to be converted to treasure. Whether it is piñon needles harvested for potpourri, wild herbs bound together for a fragrant firestarter, or fruit tree prunings chipped for aromatic barbecue fuel, these gleanings can become income instead of compost for the enterprising farmer. Chapter 4 covers the art of foraging.

Equally important to the economics of the farm is a vision that constantly seeks crop diversification. In the old days, farmers borrowed money from the bank to buy seed and tide them over until the one or at most two big crops were harvested at the end of the summer. Now crops, whether they be genetically altered roosters bred for their neck hackles beloved by fly fishermen, or specialty tomato seedlings started on hotbeds in February, are figured month by month to set up a regular cash flow and hedge against disaster hitting one particular crop. The old warning to not put all your eggs in one basket has become the rallying cry of farm advisers and farm economists all over the country.

This method of farming prescribes ingenious scheming to bring into harmonious balance a blend of livestock and produce. In France, pigs roam the orchards, cleaning up the fruitfalls and fattening themselves at the same time. Grazing sheep keep the fields clear and can be harvested for food and fleece. A sideline of breeding horses is the harvest of compostable manure, to be used as free fertilizer for the farm and to sell to backyard growers. Ducks will gobble up grasshoppers like Jujubes, and their eggs, down, and meat are all salable.

Of course, when the harvest begins to come in, it can be overwhelming, and the laws of supply and demand mean that prices in the markets drop when your crop is at the peak. Many smart farmers have turned to value-added products, harvesting the fruits and vegetables at their peak but using them later for premium products such as dried herbal blends, seeds, jams, jellies, dried vegetables, or bean blends.

Value-added products do have additional costs of processing, labeling, and storing, and the hurdles of red tape and public health regulations must be negotiated in order to bring a product to market successfully. A product's ability to keep without spoilage gives it a long shelf life, however, and unlike the perishable fresh crop, which must be taken to market as soon as it is harvested, a product can be sold all year long. Knowing what a marketing plan looks like, seeking diversified outlets for the products, following up with service, and maintaining quality are the basics for successful selling. Chapter 5 offers an in-depth look at value-added products, and Chapter 6 gives you the framework to learn how to sell them.

Living in the country gives you a special opportunity to connect with people living in the city who long for a sense of country life. These country-city connections are explored in Chapter 7.

The backyard gardening chapter (Chapter 8) gives city gardeners ideas for using the resources of small, urban spaces to farm. Chapter 9 examines the bureaucratic tangles that face farmers regardless of the size of their property, and Chapter 10 celebrates the success of farmers throughout America. You will find that the back matter provides a variety of resources for you, from superior seed companies to a crop production bibliography.

This book presents dozens of ideas for horticultural enterprises that will bring you pleasure and profit, and practical information as to how to get the most money from your work. Begin by devising a market plan that puts together a diversified crop. Research will help tailor the plan to local outlets appropriate to your product and estimate a return on your expenses. Finding distributors will help open markets beyond the local ones. Then publicity and marketing savvy will help you sell your harvest. Finally, remember that by definition, a specialty product today is old hat tomorrow; be sure to continue your market research and keep aware of the newest trends.

So put on your straw hat and join the revolution. You will find that your bank account and your satisfaction account will both benefit.

RESOURCES

Clark, Robert, ed. *Our Sustainable Table*. San Francisco: North Point Press, 1990.

An inspiring collection of essays by important figures in American agriculture on stewardship of the land.

Scher, Les. *Finding and Buying Your Place in the Country*. New York: Collier Books, Revised, 1996.

Includes everything from locating a reliable agent to researching water and timber rights.

CHAPTER 2

The Pros and Cons of Organic Farming

There is a lot of talk these days about chemical pollution, holes in the ozone layer, and deteriorating natural resources. Farmers find a lot of fingers being pointed at them as destroyers of the ecosystem, or at the very least, defilers of the groundwater and corrupters of pastures. Terms like *organic and sustainable farm systems* and *organic inputs* are tossed around with apparent authority but little clear explanation. If integrated pest management sounds to you like a far-out school for ornery children, you will appreciate the confusion growers of all sizes face in sorting out the technical jargon and advice bred by the organic-vs.-conventional controversy.

You might think that a cleaner environment and healthier food sound like two indisputably excellent goals, but on the road to being realized, they have kicked up a storm of debate and a swirl of legislative activity that have judges, lawyers, small and large farmers, grocery stores, and backyard growers pretty puzzled. Up to now, the organic industry has been governed by state regulation, with California enacting the toughest standards. Recently the federal government stepped in, devising the 1990 Organic Foods Production Act that was to have become law by October 1, 1993. The federal law would, of course, supersede the state laws; its purpose was to unify national standards. The guidelines for many regulations are not yet written, however, so the law will not take full effect until the process is completed.

In spite of this legal confusion, you can begin to look at some of the issues, in thinking about both how you want to farm and what you can afford. Backyard gardeners growing specialty lettuces in raised beds need to maintain a high level of soil fertility. Larger holdings growing seedless mini-watermelons worry about pests and mildew. Will cover crops and integrated pest management really get those melons to market? Regardless how small your holdings might be, every time you go to add something to the soil, you will be making a decision about organic farming. There are three questions you can put to yourself as a starting place for decision making.

1. Do you want to make your farm system organic, following the philosophy of growing clean food in a clean environment? Are these issues important to you?

2. Will you produce higher-quality crops in terms of taste and nutrition by avoiding synthetic chemical fertilizers and pesticides?

3. Just how much difference in your profit can farming organically mean to you? Will your customers care, and will you make money?

Let's start by looking at some of the terms that you hear in farm seminars, kitchens, and barnyards across the nation.

Certified organic. This term refers to regulations governing the use of fertilizers, pesticides, and herbicides, as well as the feed and medications given to farm animals grown for the production of meat or milk. A list of strictly proscribed materials is available from your state department of agriculture or your farm adviser. As of October 1, 1993, organic certification of land will take three years after the date of filing.

Sustainable agriculture. A farm system that uses a variety of techniques to preserve and build up the health of the soil for increased fertility and crop production without global damage. Farmers use cover crops, integrated pest management, composted animal manures, crop rotation, and a diversified production system to mimic natural biological systems. Sustainable agriculture is also called biological agriculture.

Integrated pest management. Synthetic pesticides were considered the farmer's savior when they first came into use, but a remarkable number of insects and plant diseases have become resistant to them. Farmers are also aware of the ecological damage chemical sprays do and are concerned about the effect on their health and that of their workers.

Entomologists are devising methods of encouraging beneficial insects and microorganisms that prey on these pests, keeping them under control. Farmers using IPM find that they must learn new methods of farming, from planting cover crops to creating hedgerows of certain plants that nurture beneficials, and that they must pay attention to crop conditions and pest outbreaks. IPM does use pesticides, but they are made from natural materials without long-term effects and they are deployed only in response to a specific problem.

Inputs. These are manufactured products that the farmer buys for his farm. As with any business, keeping your costs low and your production high makes money for you. Synthetic pesticides and fertilizers are costly inputs that make high yields and good sales critical to balance costs with income. Sustainable farm systems try to minimize inputs by recycling farm products for maximum efficiency and minimum waste while increasing soil fertility and therefore production.

Compost. Organic materials decompose, and when added to the soil, they improve soil composition and encourage beneficial microorganisms. Composted materials are one of the ways farmers increase the fertility of their soil without the expense and side effects of chemical fertilizers. The latest studies cite soil condition as the key element in maximum crop production; compost is an effective way to maintain the health of soil.

Organic fertilizers. Soil fertility is critical to production, and when farmers need to add fertilizers, in addition to animal manures, they use organic wastes such as bone meal and blood meal, minerals like rock phosphate and basalt dust, and guano products.

Cover crops. Agricultural practices change over time, and one of the biggest changes has been in the development of cover crops as a farm system that inhibits soil erosion, increases fertility, and enhances biological controls. However, like many innovations in agriculture, this one harks back to old-fashioned farm techniques.

There are many different types and uses of cover crops. Soybeans, fava beans, clovers, oats, and rye are harvested and plowed in to compost in the soil, or cut to decompose on top of the soil.

Certain members of the pea family, the legumes, have the ability to absorb nitrogen from the air and process it into little nodules on their roots. When harvested and allowed to decompose, these nodules of nitrogen are released back into the soil, replacing the need for fertilizer.

Cover crops also keep down weeds, reducing the need for herbicides. Some cover crops are grown for feed, and grazing livestock naturally add manure to the soil. Certain beneficial insects are attracted to plants used in cover crops as a part of an IPM system.

FARMING AND ITS GLOBAL IMPLICATIONS

Farmers are quick to point out that they are not the only ones polluting the planet. City commuters inching forward with their exhausts pumping out fumes and riverside factories spewing industrial wastes are certainly keeping them company. Growers have become aware of the public's concern about the effects of pesticides, however.

The alar alarm of 1985 proved to both organic and conventional farmers that public opinion is quick to judge, with or without understanding, and farmers bear the economic consequences. Alar is a widely used chemical sprayed onto red apples. A public furor arose when the Natural Resources Defense Council sued to prohibit growers from using the spray, citing animal studies that showed the chemical, daminozide, was a carcinogen. The NRDC was particularly concerned that babies who were eating applesauce and drinking apple juice were more vulnerable to the chemical than adults. Even movie stars got involved, making statements on television. Consumption of all apples dropped dramatically, ruining sales of small and large apple growers indiscriminantly, regardless of their chemical use or apple variety. The firestorm of controversy made it plain that health issues and agricultural practices are of great concern to the buying public.

Organic farmers challenge the conventional farming systems because they are concerned about the sustainability of both their own land and the entire earth. Desertification, pest resistance to normal dosages of deadly poisons, droughts resulting from deforestation, and populations forced into cities because of soil infertility are all realities organic farmers see as byproducts of conventional farming methods. Organic farmers believe that fertilizing with chemicals and blasting everything with pesticides and herbicides do not work with nature's own carefully balanced biological organization. They look for natural systems such as worms to aerate the soil, cover crops to put nitrogen back into the ground, biological controls to attack agricultural pests, and low-input methods to make the soil and plants healthy and productive.

Pesticide and herbicide regulation and food safety issues will be hotly debated for years to come. Scientists who deride the concern about pesticides state that residues found in food are too small to be of medical concern or have a physiological impact. Other scientists maintain that residues accumulating in our bodies are not measured in children, only adults, and the increasing incidence of cancer in children may be related to pesticide use. Controversy has erupted about whether different pesticides used on the same fruit may combine as more deadly compounds, unknown and untested.

There is no doubt that pesticides in fruits and vegetables do make people sick. In 1985, over 1,000 people were poisoned through eating watermelons that had been improperly dosed with a pesticide not registered for use on watermelons. You, the grower, must also think about your own health. Storing and applying poisons require safety equipment and a careful reading of the label.

Synthetic fertilizers are high in nitrogen, but the chemical formula is harsh on soil life, rich in microscopic bacteria. These fertilizers can kill the soil, and the nitrates pollute the groundwater. Organic farming systems recycle animal and farm wastes to create nitrogen-rich compost that is added to the soil to increase fertility and improve soil composition. They also use cover crops for nitrogen fixing, and crop rotation. These systems may be more work than opening a bag, but their practitioners are convinced that they inexpensively renew and improve soil fertility, and actually increase production.

ORGANIC VS. SUSTAINABLE

There is some confusion in the alternative-farming ranks about what defines *organic* and what defines *sustainable*. Leaders in the movement debate the vocabulary and write articles on the terminology. Basically, organic farming is a system using diversified crops, crop rotation to protect the soil, on-farm nutrients instead of synthetics, and cover cropping and biological controls to handle weed and pest problems. These methods mimic natural ecosystems, working with nature, not against it. This type of farming also reduces a farm's overhead by eliminating expensive, purchased pesticides and herbicides from the budget. Practitioners also believe their soils improve and their food is guaranteed to be healthy and nourishing.

Sustainable farming utilizes the organic farming systems; some growers, however, may use a limited amount of synthetic chemicals for things such as weed control and fertilizer. Many sustainable farmers are proud to sell their food as pesticide-free, and do not attempt to label it organic. Sustainable growers feel they have made choices that work to balance their stewardship of the land with common sense and good business practices.

Enid Wonnacott, state coordinator of the Natural Organic Farmers Association of Vermont, stated in the *Organic Farmer* magazine that sustainable farming is "ecologically sound, economically viable, and socially responsible."

IS THE QUALITY OF ORGANIC BETTER?

In the late 1970s, when organic produce began to appear in supermarkets, consumers grumbled because it was not perfect. Lettuce leaves were ratty, with holes from hungry pests, and apples did not shine from wax applications. Consumers repelled by bugs in the broccoli often chose to return to regular produce. Added to the problems of quality was the produce manager's bias. Organic produce was placed in the most inconspicuous part of the section. Consequently, when organic did not sell, produce managers said the consumer was not interested.

Most retailers feel that the alar event changed all that. The quality of organic produce, vastly improved over the last ten years, is now excellent, both in appearance and substance, so when panicky consumers turned to the organic alternative they found it palatable. Now that we are several years away from the alar brouhaha, some buyers have gone back to their old ways, buying less expensive, nonorganic produce, but many consumers have not. In fact, many have switched totally to organic, preferring the taste and wanting to reduce the risks they perceive may exist in eating nonorganic.

The flavor issue continues to be debated. The same variety of tomato will taste different when grown in different locations of the country because of soil and climate variables. Organic farmers say that organic food tastes better, because chemical fertilizers diminish the flavor. A taste test run by the Department of Food Science at Rutgers University found no huge differences, but the tasters pointed out that the organically grown tomatoes were slightly sweeter, and less bitter and acidic.

WILL GROWING ORGANIC REAP HIGHER RETURNS?

Farm production under organic systems may be more expensive because farmers eschew quick-fix chemical solutions for more labor-intensive farming practices. People who want to buy organic produce are willing to pay more for it. Distributors expect a 10 to 25 percent premium on organic produce, so growers get more money for their products. (Remember, of course, that the law of supply and demand is operating, so if organic growers increase in number, these prices may drop.) Specialty crops bring higher prices, but organic specialty crops top those. There is a definite advantage at the cash register. Some farmers' markets work only with growers of organic produce. These markets have a reputation for handling the finest organic fruits and vegetables, and chefs, wholesalers, and retailers stroll the markets to locate sources for their businesses.

The *Gourmet Retailer,* a magazine for merchants of specialty food, notes that more and more organic processed products are reaching the store shelves. A lengthy article for a special edition given away at the 1992 Fancy Food Show profiles the specialty food shopper who will buy organic with a sense of balancing unhealthy food with healthy food. The magazine points out that this "having your cake and eating your vegetables too" attitude will increase when the Organic Foods Protection Act goes into effect, because more buyers will be aware of organic.

In both processed and fresh goods, the demand is growing but the supply is limited, a situation that will keep organic produce highly marketable for a number of years to come. The number of organic processors is growing, and there are indications that major international food companies are in the middle of product development to come out with totally organic lines of food for babies and toddlers.

Bu Nygens of Veritable Vegetable, a distributor in San Francisco who sells organic produce, finds demand increasing steadily. More and more smaller chain supermarkets are opening organic produce sections, she notes. Although prices for organic produce may vary slightly both up and down depending on the product, Bu expects the standard guidelines for pricing to remain 20 percent over conventional produce. Her major problem is finding enough consistent suppliers to fill her orders and keep the prices stable. Bu advises organic growers to go through the process of getting certified.

CERTIFICATION

When the new federal law goes into effect with the rules promulgated leading to full implementation, probably by summer of 1997, all farmers with annual sales of more than $5,000 must have their land certified organic before beginning to sell products as organic. Until that law does go into effect, state regulations prevail, so check with your state agricultural department for their certification programs. Be aware that the federal program will enforce a three-year waiting period before your land can be certified organic. Get started as soon as possible: Check with your county advisor to find out what the process entails in your state.

Pesticide Regulation

All synthetically produced pesticides are prohibited for use on your land. There are some natural pesticides that may be applied, made from plants such as nicotine and pyrethrum. Certain oils are allowed as sprays. If you have animals on the farm, you will need to give them only organic feeds and medications. Again, there are some exceptions for certain situations, so become fully informed by checking with the Department of Agriculture.

Fertilizer Regulation

Organic fertilizers such as composted horse, chicken, or turkey manure are allowed for nitrogen enrichment. Cover crops of legumes and certain grains will put nitrogen back into the soil. State by state, exceptions are made for certain synthetic fertilizers, in particular those that supply certain trace elements of minerals.

Postharvest Handling

Most states have regulations regarding how the produce is handled once it is off the tree or out of the ground and on its way to market. Chemicals in

postharvest rinses and fungicides in waxes may not
be allowable, so you will need to check.

Labeling

If you are a certified organic grower, you must label
all your products correctly. According to federal
standards, you need to state that your products
meet the Department of Agriculture standards for
organic production. Labeling will be required on individual packages and on standard boxes.

Paperwork

Each state is different, but many certification programs call for filing a variety of farm information
such as a map of your property with crops listed,
the kinds of pesticides you have used, the quantities, the crops you applied pesticides to, the amount
of each crop grown, and your gross annual sales, to
mention just a few items.

Certification Organizations

Part of the pending federal Organic Foods Production Act requires certification by an accredited organization. These organizations visit farms and
work with growers to familiarize them with all the
regulations and paperwork. In some cases, the accreditation organization charges a fee; in others, a
percentage is taken yearly based on your sales volume. These latter groups see themselves as lobby-
ists, working with legislatures and publishing
materials to help the farmer receive added sales.
Just how the accreditation groups work will be
further defined by the Act guidelines that are now
in preparation.

ORGANIZATIONS OF ORGANIC FARMERS

Numerous groups have formed to help explore alternative farming methods, from organic to sustainable. They have bushels of publications, pamphlets, magazines, and good information to get you started growing organically. The Annual Ecological Farming Conference that is held every year in California is one of the largest conferences on organic growing methods in America. It offers workshops on everything from organic cotton to on-farm research to biotechnology. A number of other sustainable-agriculture conferences take place all over the country, and they are a proven place to learn some of the newest techniques and to share experiences with other farmers. Most of these conferences take place in January and February, off-season time. The *Organic Farmer* and other farm periodicals and newsletters usually carry listings; check with the Internet or your local farm advisor.

If you go to the library and consult magazines about organic farming, you will find lots of information on groups in your region. See the reference listing to online sources (page 192) as well. Several universities have alternative-farming programs, such as the University of California, Davis's Small Farm Center and Cornell University's Alternative Farming Program. Either of these organizations can refer you to groups working in your area.

RESOURCES

Bainbridge, David, and Steve Mitchel. *Sustainable Agriculture for California: A Guide for Information.* Oakland: UC Sustainable Agriculture Research and Education Program, University of California, Division of Agriculture and Natural Resources, Publication 3349, 1991.

California Certified Organic Farmers
115 Mission Street
Santa Cruz, CA 95060
831/423-2263

They will refer you to an organic organization in your area.

Holistic Management, Allan Savoy Center for
1010 Tiejeras NW
Albuquerque, NM 87102
800/654-3619

A revolutionary approach to farm systems management.

Mid-West Organic Alliance
http://www.organic.org

The National Organic Directory
CAFF
P.O. Box 464
Davis, CA 95617
530/756-8518

Organic Farmers Marketing Association
http://www.iquest.net/ofma

Organic Gardening Magazine
Rodale Press
33 East Minor Street
Emmaus, PA 18098
215/967-5171
One of the most respected publications in the field.

Organic Farming Research Foundation
Bob Scowcroft, Executive Director
P.O. Box 440
Santa Cruz, CA 95061
831/426-6606

Accepting research proposals on organic methods.

Organic Growers Source Book and Catalog
Peaceful Valley Farm Supply
P.O. Box 2209
Grass Valley, CA 95945
888/784-1722

CHAPTER 3

Growing Specialty Vegetables and Herbs

The French intensive method of growing vegetables and fruits, the engineering of raised beds, and drip irrigation—breakthroughs pioneered and written about by John Jeavons, Eliot Coleman, and a host of other enthusiasts—have revolutionized the production of food in America, from families privately enjoying and renewing gardening traditions to entrepreneurs turning city lots into truck farms that reap hundreds of thousands of dollars every year.

What was then called the French intensive method now has many different names, but it is basically a system of carefully tending and enriching the soil and planting closely, or intensively, for maximum production. Growers and farmers find the time they put into soil work and seeding and thinning to maintain the beds thickly covered with fruits and vegetables brings a payback far in excess of what conventional growing methods would produce.

Alan Chadwick, an Englishman who taught at the University of California, Santa Cruz, in the 1960s and 1970s, had a garden that looked unlike anything seen in agriculture at that time. Instead of rows of vegetables, he dug up beds of soil, raising them into neat mounds, and he totally covered them with plants.

Eschewing the normal techniques of cultivation, he mixed in compost and organic fertilizers and dug into his soil twelve inches deep, carefully working in the organic materials.

Instead of overhead sprinklers, you now see spaghetti tubes of drip irrigation systems running throughout gardens and garden beds. Drip systems deliver water in small, steady doses, just the way the plant likes it. Drip irrigation has gone hand in hand with raised beds to allow a very efficient, successful watering to maximize production while minimizing labor.

Michael Norton of Kona Kai Gardens in Berkeley, California, led the way in demonstrating these progressive methods. His miniature production farm on a corner lot in the middle of a small commercial section of town should be registered in the annals of agricultural history. Bus tours actually pass by his lot to admire the neat configuration of raised beds that grow specialty lettuces in colors from chartreuse to bronzy red. During the years of peak production in the 1980s, that four-tenths of an acre grossed $238,000 a year. Norton sold to a variety of white-tablecloth restaurants, to walk-in shoppers on Saturdays, and air shipped to Japan and Hong Kong.

On an even smaller scale, Stephanie Delmont of D&M Gardens in Orinda, California, grows specialty lettuce, herbs, and eggplants in raised beds in her city-size backyard, earning almost $5,000 every year as an adjunct to her other business. She figures she cultivates raised beds of 1,200 square feet of lettuce, 1,800 feet of herbs in her front yard, plus some eggplants in containers. This plan works successfully for her because she plans her beds carefully, continually rotating her lettuce and stretching production out over the long, mild summer.

DIVERSIFIED PRODUCTION

In contrast to these operations, American agriculture has been dominated by huge farms, both family owned and corporate owned. Large-acreage farms developed in the Midwest when land was cheap and crop prices were cheaper. Only by having a lot of land and growing a big crop was it possible to survive. Mechanization and pesticides have worked together to foster farms that cash in on one or two huge crops a year, but that system, as we have seen during the recession, has put a lot of farmers out of business, and their farms on the auction block.

Smaller farmers have looked to other models; one of the most striking successes is the Amish people still farming in America today as their forebears did a hundred years ago. The Amish run their farms at a profit. They work hard to limit the cost of inputs by recycling, composting, and using what they have at hand, and they diversify their products for a year-round harvest. In short, like any well-run business, they work to keep their overhead and operating expenses low, create products that they can sell all year long, and look for a number of different markets to make sure they sell all they make or grow.

Learning from the Amish, small farmers and growers are working with farm advisers to come up with a system of farm production that harks back to market garden days, and its success has been remarkable enough that even the large-acreage farmers are beginning to take notice. This system, called diversified production, involves a carefully calculated succession of different crops planted throughout the year to ensure a steady harvest. When possible, woven into the planting system is an animal husbandry program that produces homegrown fertilizer, helps keep down weeds, and contributes to family food or market production. As an adjunct to the system, rotation with cover crops ensures soil fertility in small growing areas, because the cover crops have special nitrogen-fixing properties, returning fertility to the soil when cut and plowed back into it. Joining the mix of harvested fresh crops that are part of a diversified production system are value-added products. Value-added products such as jams, dried herb blends, and decorative items use farm labor efficiently in the non-growing season and provide a steady cash flow for the farm.

Smaller part-time farmers have adapted this same system, combining early-producing varieties to start off the season with later-season varieties to extend the harvest. Intensive growing uses space very efficiently utilizing such techniques as intercropping early-harvest lettuce with later-producing crops that will grow into the space left when the lettuce has gone to market. The timing of planting successive crops may be tricky to start, but after one season, most producers soon have the knack of how to keep their soil and market stalls full over a very long season.

INTENSIVE GROWING

As a market gardener, whether you have less than 2,000 square feet or two acres, you need to carefully calculate your planting to maximize your production. Sit down and draw up a month-by-month planting chart, and then figure how you can squeeze in the greatest amount of variety through planting techniques and use of seasonal varieties.

Most crops have different varieties that mature at different rates. *Early, mid-season,* and *late-season* are terms used to describe the time a plant takes from planting or transplanting until ready to harvest. If you plant different varieties with different maturity dates, you can extend your harvest from early to late in the season.

Intercropping is mixing quickly harvested crops with those that take a longer time. You can plant early-harvesting varieties with later varieties, pulling out the early varieties to leave space for the longer-developing plants to grow into maturity. You can also plant thickly, making room by harvesting some plants early as tender "baby vegetables." Many people prefer the small, pencil-size leek to the two-inch variety.

Use areas left for proper spacing between mature plants that will not be needed until those plants grow bigger. Radishes that almost pop out of the ground, harvesting in 24 to 35 days, can be planted between the specialty crop daikon, or Japanese, radishes that take up to 55 days. Tomatoes hogging bed space as adults are spindly babies, leaving room for early lettuce or annual herbs such as dill. Celeriac takes 110 days to grow into its mature size, giving you lots of time to interplant with quicker-harvesting baby turnips that should be out of the ground before the temperature goes over 80 degrees.

Another way to strategize your planting space is to look closely at the harvest dates of the plants you grow. Planting early, mid-season, and late-season tomatoes will give you the longest stretch for harvest, but even so, you can modify your plan for extra rewards. Early determinate tomatoes produce one crop quickly, and after harvest, you can then pull out those plants and start fall crops in that space.

In hot climates, lettuce is unhappy unless it has some mixed shade to protect it from the sun. Smart planners sow lettuce seeds underneath corn, sunflowers, or other tall plants.

Even if you have plenty of land, try some of the techniques used by growers who are pinched for space. Trellises or fences for melon and cucumber vines leave you extra space for herbs or test plots for new varieties you want to experiment with. Tomatoes grow better staked or trained up than when left to sprawl over the ground.

Urban gardeners make very good use of containers, and even full-time farmers might consider them as an option to maximize their production. Tender herbs and plants prey to slugs, snails, and birds can be protected better in containers. Mint, which will take over beds, will be disciplined out of its bad habits. Containers are a great way to start plants to transplant when your beds are free from a previous harvest, again increasing your production capability.

Making the most of your space takes time and practice. Improve your harvest by keeping a production diary, and make sure you write in planting days, varieties, quantities, days to harvest, successes, and—equally important—failures. Only by experimenting will you come up with a good formula that works for you, and having a written planting history can be a guidebook to your success.

WHAT IS A SPECIALTY CROP?

The rule of thumb defines it as a crop that is not a commodity; one that is grown in small quantities.

This relative rarity is part of what makes it special, and of course the supply-and-demand rule means prices will be high. Commodities are fruits and vegetables recognized by the mainstream produce industry and sold in bulk.

Specialty crops aren't just unusual varieties of fruits and vegetables, but ordinary ones that become available at an unusual time in the season—the first in, or the last. If you have an orchard, being first to market with your peaches will make them highly desirable and your customers will be beating a path to your stall.

Specialty crops can also be an unusual harvesting of a normal crop. Most farmers harvest squash as mature vegetables, for example, but those who pick them as baby vegetables can sell them at a specialty price. Baby vegetables are in demand because they are so sweet and tender. Do not confuse this with a product like haricots verts, beans that are tiny when they are fully grown. Some miniature corns are also fully ripe when picked; they are tiny by nature, hence they're special.

Another area of specialty crops is the exotics used in certain ethnic cuisines. Pea tendrils are sought after as a Chinese culinary delicacy extremely difficult to find in ordinary markets. Bitter melons, the long white radish called a daikon, and many unusual types of eggplant are also popular in Asian communities. Thai and Indian cuisines need unusual varieties of basil, mint, eggplants, and chilies for their distinctive dishes. Working with restaurateurs to produce these crops can introduce the grower to new specialties. The popularity of spicy Hispanic food is rising all over the country. A variety of herbs and spices perfect for the specialty grower are used in large quantities daily in restaurants and homes everywhere. Tomatillos, used for green salsas, are small, papery-husked fruits that grow as easily as cherry tomatoes. Cilantro is a hardy leafy herb used both in Mexican and Asian cuisines. You can easily produce a value-added product with chili powder, which is a mix of the dried, then powdered chilies.

The important point to understand about a specialty crop is that it may be special today, but with marketplace acceptance, it will be run of the mill tomorrow. Those people who grew Granny Smith apples in the 1980s as a specialty crop found that the price dropped as the supply of Grannies swelled; it is clear that Grannies are no longer a specialty crop. Gizdich Ranch, in Watsonville, California, planted Grannies when they first became available. Now they face the tough decision to stop growing Grannies and switch to growing Braeburns, the newest specialty apple. They found that their U-pick crowd does not view Grannies with any interest, and they have been forced to use their apples in pies and juice as a way to use the crop.

As a small farmer, you have the flexibility to stay on top of market trends. The big farmers with hundreds of acres of crops will sell for volume through the commodities market, their success based on the amount they can sell. Your modest size allows you to work the market to your best advantage.

SPECIALTY CROP SELECTION

Research is your first money-making tool, and it can take lots of different guises. At a recent farm conference, one of the speakers flatly announced that the best and cheapest market research study she ever did was simply asking her customers what they wanted, and then listening to their responses. One farmer in Arizona spent nights looking through all the seed catalogs when a customer mentioned a seedless watermelon that had a great flavor. The next summer, that farmer was the first one in the area selling seedless watermelons, and the prices were premium.

Frieda Caplan of Frieda's Finest Produce Specialties in Los Angeles, a leader in introducing new crops to the wholesale market, suggests the following steps when you are ready to launch a new crop:

1. Determine what can grow in your soil, given your climate and water availability. Your local cooperative extension farm adviser and the Soil Conservation Service can help you assess your land and climate's potential.

2. Talk to a good seed company to find out what seed or plant stock is available and what varieties the company recommends (see Seed Sources, page 185).

3. Talk to distributors to see whether a market for your crop exists.

4. Once you've done all of the above, experiment with the crop by planting a small plot or a few rows to get some experience.

5. Be sure to plan how the product is to be packed and shipped. Does it need to be culled and/or cleaned? What postharvest handling and standard packs are required?

Specialty crops, by definition, must be handled as gently as eggs. Most farmers pick the evening or morning before they go to market, to be sure that their products are at the very peak of their ripeness, so their taste and texture are fully developed.

Getting Your Customers to Buy It

You may spend long agonizing hours poring over seed catalogs, plan your cropping systems and market delivery dates carefully, and discover the old maxim about leading a horse to water, although you wouldn't want to describe your customers as ornery nags. There are times when you make choices based on a variety of factors, such as growing conditions, farm adviser recommendations, and your land, but you find your buyers do not appreciate your farsightedness.

Patti Adams of Adams Station Produce in Gasquet, California, found that she had to work to get her customers to taste and then buy the new varieties of tomatoes she was growing that were particularly well suited to the local climate. The taste of the Tigerella was wonderful, but its stripes made it look peculiar. After some persuasion and free samples, customers did try it—and then grumbled when they sold out. Adams had the same problem introducing Golden Jubilee corn. She had to grow old-fashioned varieties with inferior flavor because her customers demanded them, and she won over customers to the better-tasting variety only by giving away free ears of it. Now, her entire clientele has switched, and all the corn grown at Adams Station is Golden Jubilee.

HERBS

One of the largest growth industries in agriculture is herbs—for nursery stock, culinary uses, herbal teas, and the newest outlet, the alternative medicine and pharmaceutical trade.

Although most of us think we know what herbs

are generally, there is actually a wide variety of plants classified as herbs. Some are grown for seed, others for leaf, bark, or roots. Although usually the least bothersome of plants in their care requirements, some herbs are reported to adjust to climate and soil with different growth habits, so what flourishes like a weed in dry California summers will react differently in humid South Carolina. Many of the plants raised in America originated in Mediterranean climates, so freezing cold is against their nature and they must be protected and mulched. Herbs mature in various ways, with annuals growing to harvest quickly from seed, some perennials developing into small trees or shrubs, and biennials growing and going to seed within two years. Ginseng, one of the most lucrative herbs to cultivate for export, takes up to ten years to become profitable, and it is extremely difficult to propagate.

There is a romance and tradition to herbs, and their fragrant leaves and the host of bees and hummingbirds they attract make them a great favorite of growers. On warm summer days, the sun seems to lift a gentle scent from the plants, and lining garden paths with herbs encourages the garden stroller to pluck a leaf. Rolling the leaf between your fingers brings the sensual pleasure of the aroma, although with some herbs that are an insect repellent, the experience will be startlingly pungent. A glance at bookstore shelves will show that books about herbs outnumber those on any other topic in the garden section.

As an adjunct to a farm operation or a sideline in a backyard plot, herbs can provide a steady income. You will see farmers in the summer markets selling fresh cut herbs or starts for the home gardener. In France, baskets planted with fresh herbs line the sidewalks of the garden stalls, and green garlic,

garlic bulbs, shallots, and cut herbs are a major part of every produce store.

Culinary Herbs

Culinary herbs have been around to season stews, pickle vegetables, scent jellies, and garnish salads as long as chefs have been stirring pots. Professionals and home cooks alike chop fresh herbs for their full flavor and bright specks of color instead of reaching for jars of dried or powdered herbs, which have the tendency to hang around long after the taste has gone. Supermarkets that used to sell only rubber-banded bouquets of curled parsley now stock baskets with little bundles of fresh summer savory, tarragon, rosemary, silver thyme, lemon thyme, and dill.

Some herbs are tough perennials, others are tender annuals. If you are growing culinary herbs, you need to follow your same checklist of research and development as you did when you were designing your specialty vegetable cropping system to arrive at a list of herbs that will yield a profit given your soil, climate, and market. Consider the possibilities of using herbs to extend your growing season by drying and bottling them and making herbal vinegar and wreaths. Seeds of certain varieties of herbs can be sold at a premium, both for propagation and for cooking. Sesame seeds, seeds of the nigella flower, poppyseeds, and dill are all used in cooking. Specialty bakeries like to scatter seeds on loaf tops.

The Herbal Medicine Market

Can you imagine what codeine, morphine, ephedrine, quinine, digitalis, and curare have in common?

They are all plant-derived drugs actively pre-
scribed by doctors today. Brother Cadfael, the
herbalist in the novels by Ellis Peters set in the
1100s, describes a walled monastery garden on a
warm summer day filled with the smells of healing
plants and the sounds of browsing bumblebees.
Herbalists were the first doctors. Herbal remedies
form the basis of nontraditional medical practices
that are as old as humankind. The seemingly om-
nipotent wonders of modern medicine obscured for
some time the real and useful role of herbs as a
companion to lifelong health, but recent discoveries
involving the chemistry of herbal properties and
their medicinal effectiveness have increased the
awareness of the medical community. Funding for
research is sorely lacking, but from a state of de-
cline, herbs' medical stature and economic importance are reaching new heights today.

In 1993, the National Institutes of Health opened
the Office of Alternative Medicine, which will
begin to solicit research proposals on herbal medicines and other alternative healing systems. This is
a major step, because there is much confusion in
consumers' minds about herbal prescriptions. Although in Canada no health claims can be made on
a label without a DIN (drug identification number),
and no criteria govern the manufacture of natural
products, in America there are some guidelines for
certain herbs. Regulations *are* crucial because different species of herbs have different chemical com-
positions, and of course affect the body differently.
Taking herbal remedies seriously enough to test for
chemical composition, to regulate manufacturers,
and to maintain strict label laws will legitimize herbal medicines and spur research to learn how herbs
work to cure bodily ills.

A number of alternatives to conventional medicine use herbs. Chinese medicine combines several different curing methods, including acupuncture and herbs, to address the total body system. Among the medications homeopathic practitioners employ are plant extracts. American Indians collect, dry, and use a variety of natural products in teas, salves, and potions to cure mind and body.

Herbal Teas

In 1970, Celestial Seasonings, a small company making teas in Denver, Colorado, began to package and market unusual herbal teas throughout the western states. Now an international company, they buy herbs from local farmers and importers. Other tea companies have sprung up as the benefits of caffeine-free beverages have gained public awareness. Some of these teas, like Traditional Medicinals of Healdsburg, California, do make medical claims according to the published guidelines of the FDA; others exist for the pleasure of their flavor. Take time to investigate the possibility of growing herbs for some of these companies. Celestial Seasonings buys dried, sacked herbs from farmers, with a 2,000-pound minimum, but other companies may be interested in working with you.

Some companies say they have had difficulty working with farmers, and that it is easier for them to buy directly from brokers. This is a shame. Here is an expanding market that is being filled to a great extent through import. If you want to grow and sell herbs to these companies, remember that they will require reliability from you; they do not want to spend their time and money working with you if you are going to vanish after a couple of years. This kind of customer is different from chefs and farmers' markets because of the large amounts most companies demand. Requirements also include drying the herbs, and delivery to specification. Some herbs are delivered as dried leaves, flowers, or roots, so labor is involved in the processing.

Companies do say they are interested in setting up relationships to buy smaller quantities. Before you leap into this endeavor, investigate and research prices for finished herbs, ease of processing, and drying methods. (If you live in a damp climate, drying herbs may not be practical and you should stick to selling fresh.) There are also groups of buyers who will buy smaller quantities from farmers, picking up a couple of pounds at a time from a central distributor.

NICHE MARKETING

Niche marketing is a term that is thrown around carelessly in the press, but is rarely defined or explained. All it means is finding a special product, selling something no one else is selling, or selling something where no one else has thought of it as a product. The image of a niche is a small shelf along the side of a cliff. There is room for only a very limited number of products on the niche—too many, and something falls off the shelf. Specialty produce and herbs are naturals for niche marketing because of their limited supply and superb quality. A small but loyal clientele is willing to pay bonus prices because of those characteristics.

Growing Thai basil and selling directly to Asian markets and restaurants is an example of niche marketing. Seeking a marmalade producer that uses only organic fruit and growing specifically for that producer is another example.

Being eager to cultivate new products, open new markets, and make it easy for your customers to use them is important if your market strategy is to go after a niche that is unoccupied by your competition. Growers trying to break into the niche market need to be very flexible in their planning, because everyone notices a good thing, and if you have the newest gunmetal blue winter squash to show up in the market, or an unusual European melon, chances are next year the market will be full of those squash and melons, and your prices will drop.

Quality Sells

The size of Stephanie Delmont's gardens should point out that you do not have to cultivate acres to make money. It is more important to produce a small amount of a quality product than huge quantities with little or no flavor. Every successful small farmer today will tell you that quality sells. Quality means a product that looks good and tastes good. Quality also means the kind of business practices you use. Good salespeople like the products they sell, know about them—from the best way to store to different ways to prepare—and they like engaging their customers and educating them about the things they are selling.

RESOURCES

Hill, Lewis. *Christmas Trees: Growing and Selling Trees, Wreaths, and Greens.* Wownal, Vt.: Garden Way Publishing, 1989.

Growing for Market
News and Ideas for Market Gardeners
P.O. Box 3747
Lawrence, KS 66046
800/307-8949
www.growingformarket.com

This monthly newsletter comes jammed with topics e.g., how to start a processed food business, CSAs, regulation of salad mix, and the controversy over the sale of the seeds of *Papaver soniferum*, the opium poppy.

Kourik, Robert. *Designing and Maintaining Your Edible Landscape Naturally.* Santa Rosa: Metamorphic Press,1986.

Larkcom, Joy. *Oriental Vegetables: The Complete Guide for Garden and Kitchen.* New York: Kodansha International, 1991.
Excellent gardening guide with cultivation and variety information.

Reich, Lee. *Uncommon Fruits Worthy of Attention: A Gardener's Guide.* Reading, Mass.: Addison-Wesley, 1991.
A thorough examination of unusual fruits for the market garden.

Roger Yepsen, Jr. *Growing for Market: A Guide to Producing and Marketing Vegetables, Fruit, Honey, Herbs, Beef, Cheese, Mushrooms, Wine, Woolen Goods, and More.* Emmaus, Pa.: Rodale Press, 1978.

Herbs

Business of Herbs
Northwind Farm, Route 2
Box 246
Shevlin, MN 56676-9535
Subscription $24 per year for bimonthly journal.
This journal contains trade news, marketing hints, and trade resources.

A Gardener's Source Guide
P.O. Box 206
Gowanda,.NY 14070
Lists mail order companies that offer free catalogs.

The Herb Companion
201 East Fourth Street
Loveland, CO 80537
Subscription $24 per year for bimonthly magazine
A magazine for hobbyists and more serious growers. Excellent classified ad section.

CHAPTER 4

Treasures: Foraging for Profit

People who own woods and pastures, or weekend naturalists who like to spend time outdoors have the opportunity to bring in extra cash by foraging. Traditionally, foraging has meant collecting wild things to sell, but this chapter expands that concept to include planting things that go wild or grow wildly, recycling ordinary farm products such as prunings or compost, and scavenging a variety of postproduction crops, from cornstalks to rosehips.

If you have your own farm or land, you can start foraging by walking out your back door. If you're a backyard grower, your opportunities are a bit more limited, but not impossible. Get into the habit of scavenging things about to be thrown out at the farmers' market, be on the lookout for products you can make, and ask other sellers with large acreage whether you can come to their land. Check out national forests that are close to your home.

THE PLEASURES OF NATURAL PRODUCTS

City dwellers who live with cement sidewalks instead of meadows and tall buildings instead of trees are looking for ways to bring some nature into their urban existence. Wreaths can brighten living rooms, kitchens, and even bedrooms all year long, surrounding us with good smells and the subtle textures and colors of the outdoors. Potpourri from evergreens, herbs, and nuts brings the fragrant and sensual suggestion of the wild. Twenty stories up in a city apartment, these little touches satisfy an essential longing for nature's presence.

Many natural decorative items sold in the city, such as bouquets of dried seed pods, bowls filled with acorns and pine cones, and candles poured into oak galls, are made from bits and pieces of plants that are literally lying around on your farmland. The old adage "One person's trash is another's treasure" holds true for more than garage sales. Looking for ways to glean from your land and thereby diversify your income can be as exciting as any treasure hunt.

In order to come up with what you might forage from your property, think like the ultimate recycler. First, inventory your possible resources. Ask yourself what you throw out that you might sell instead. Look for things that you pay to have hauled away or you have to work to dispose of. Do you have compostable materials? Do you have aromatic prunings that others would want for smoking or barbecuing? What part of your crops do you plow under that just might be gleaned for sale if harvested, dried, and processed in some unusual way?

Florists need greens, berries, leaves, nuts, acorns, and pine cones. Every spring, pussy willow branches sell in flower shops, and for many farmers these trees grow like weeds. Cattails are a decorative item in many homes, and the leaves, called rush, are also used in caning chairs. Branches with baby wild persimmons make beautiful floral displays, and the wood is related to ebony. Bowls crafted from burls sell for hundreds of dollars.

If you live on a farm, use the less busy times to prepare and sell foraged items. Foraging often dovetails with the farm's off-season: fall and winter are the times to prepare dried grasses picked when their seedpods were plump and hung upside-down to dry, to cut and tie greens for holiday wreaths, and to finish mixing the potpourri. During those seasons, fall leaf displays and cherry-red berries are at their peak, mistletoe spotting is easy, and it's time for fruit tree pruning. *Land cruising,* an old-fashioned term used by turn-of-the-century foresters, is a grand excuse for family treks over your property to discover possible materials for sale.

RESEARCHING AND MARKETING THE PRODUCT

Figure out what might sell from your scavenging. The alchemist's trick of turning garbage into gold relies on your ability to find out what the market wants to buy and then uncovering what you have that matches. Develop relationships with potential clients and ask them what they want and when they want it delivered. Sometimes florists will order plain green wreaths that they decorate in their own particular signature style. Other florists located near wholesale brokers prefer to buy greens from them, but they are looking for unusual materials such as dried seedpods or berries not sold by the big suppliers—or sold only in large quantities—to finish off their designs. Florists making everlasting wreaths from pine cones and nuts may want supplies delivered in July to allow plenty of time to have the goods ready for Christmas.

Besides just figuring out what you have and how much you can supply, make sure your product brings home a profit by factoring in the time it takes you to gather, package, label, and market or deliver. Packaging makes your product shelf-worthy, but involves expenses of materials and time. Sometimes you can make a better profit by harvesting and delivering just the raw goods.

Learning the Market

Your possibilities are limited only by the market's interest, but that is hard to figure. How is anyone to know what the fickle public will want next? Wreaths from grape prunings, bay leaves, and herbs are big this year, but will they be next year? Pine needle sachets wrapped in lace sell out in gift shops this season, but what if they are out of fashion next year? Can wild forest potpourri sell out at Christmas yet another year? Will candles poured into birch bark rounds continue to be the gift items of choice for those "difficult to shop for" aunts and uncles?

From these questions, it is clear that selling foraged goods involves many of the same problems as selling any specialty produce crop. As illustrated by the "pet rock" phenomenon, which had one brief year as the hit gift, the market is fickle and changeable, and the only rule is that it follows no rules.

If you discover you have the knack for tuning in to new market trends, continue to experiment. If, however, you do not have the inclination, time, or skill to track the market, work with a good wholesaler, florist, or broker who will tell you what is selling and help you stay on top of the hottest trends. It does your bank account no good to create beautiful, useful products if no one wants to buy them. People working with the buying public have learned how to anticipate and assess trends, and market researchers like Faith Popcorn make their living from maximizing their seerlike skills. For the farmer, who is oftentimes far away from gift shops and business places, working with the advice of professionals is the most effective means to continue to make money.

Cultivating these relationships with your buyers is well worth the effort. Take the time to stop and talk with them. Alta Tingle of The Gardener, a gift shop in Berkeley, California, says she is always looking for people to bring her fresh or dried plants at least once a month. She prefers working with the forager to order what she wants, taking the guesswork out of the forager's job. Her favorite things bought from a forager were bundles of tall, dried okra plants with pods still on them. She stresses that she needs reliability. If she knows that the forager will call on her as dependably as her sales reps, she is delighted to establish a long-term working relationship.

When spending a day in the city, visit a wholesale flower mart early in the morning and talk to the various brokers there. Stop in all the florists' shops and ask them where the most elegant gift shops might be that feature natural materials. If you find florists who feature designs with natural materials you could furnish, ask whether they would buy from you. If they will not buy from you directly, ask them the name of their wholesaler, because the wholesaler may be interested. Be sure to set a price that covers your gathering and travel time, so you will be able to show a profit. Do not make promises you can't keep. You won't get another chance with that buyer.

ANIMAL BYPRODUCTS

A well-documented story of foraging in an urban setting is that of the San Francisco Zoo, which had been spending great amounts of money hauling away the zoo inhabitants' stall waste, until an enterprising forager named Isabelle Wade realized that there was a valuable resource being thrown out. After careful composting, she harvested "Zoo Doo," a marketing success and a money-maker for the zoo's programs. She saved the money previously spent on hauling the manure to the local dumps, and she made money selling the "end" product. Zoo Doo is marketed to home gardeners in elegant garden shops and in national catalogs. Redwood Hill Goat Dairy in Sebastopol, California, barters their goat manure with local home gardeners, receiving summer produce, bottles of wine, and even handmade wool socks as payment. A turkey farm in Cotati, California, sells composted turkey manure through a neighboring rose dealer, because turkey manure is reputed to coax out the most beautiful blooms. Gold comes in many colors and aromas.

MAPLE SYRUP

Another good example of foraging comes from the enterprising farmers in the Northeast, who have long harvested sap from their forests for maple syrup. Selling at about $15 a quart, maple syrup can provide good revenue. One innovative Massachusetts company called Rent Mother Nature has come up with a wonderful marketing angle. The company advertises a rent-a-tree program, a gift plan in which the donor "rents" a sap-bearing tree for the recipient. During the year, "renters" receive mailers with regional lore and progress reports, and in the spring, a decorated bucket of syrup arrives. Other farmers not only harvest the syrup, but also have built breakfast restaurants around maple syrup enterprises, putting the whole family to work and bringing in paying visitors to their farm.

RECYCLING WOOD

If you are tearing out an old orchard, it is worth your time to check the Yellow Pages of the nearest large town for woodworker associations or specialty wood mills. There are some 260,000 professional and amateur woodworkers in America, and you can find them in the phone book or through local schools that offer woodworking classes. Woodworker associations covet pear, walnut, cherry, grapefruit, and many other types of fruit wood that are not sold in lumberyards, and they will buy the wood and haul it away. If you are worried about liability by inviting a bunch of people on your property, check with your insurance carrier and ask the association to pay for a one-day policy. Of course, it might be easier to make a huge bonfire, but the opportunity for a weenie roast does not outweigh the opportunity to make some money, and the thought that someday your old trees might be a beautiful table or bowl adds an extra pleasure to the feel of folding money.

David Faison of the Petaluma, California, mill and business Into the Woods negotiates both with woodcutters and farmers in order to save valuable timber most farmers find more convenient to torch. He acknowledges the difficulties of persuading busy farmers to take the time to sell their orchards just because the wood is particularly beautiful and valuable to craftspeople. Faison offers twice the amount that woodcutters pay in order to save orchard wood. If he is buying directly from the woodcutter, he works with the bulldozer operator to make sure the trees are taken out at the bottom of the trunk. Sometimes, when there is only a small amount of wood to take out, he barters with the owner, returning beautiful tables from the wood of the old orchard. He mentions the difficulty of purchasing ornamentals such as the deodar cedar, plentiful in many of the drier California valleys, but often just cut down and hauled away even though the fragrance of the wood makes it a highly desirable product.

Faison suggests planting plum or cherry trees as ornamentals, then allowing them to develop a tall trunk for trunk veneer. The trees will be exceedingly valuable as timber after forty years—a long time to wait for harvest, but the trees will count as an asset to be valued should the farmer sell the farm.

WILD PLANTS

What edible plants grow wild on your land? Wild crab apples can be found all over America. Blackberries, blueberries, and exotic wild berries such as thimbleberries and salmonberries can be made into jam or sold to chefs specializing in regional cuisine. Certain chefs like to offer the emerging buds of the fiddlehead fern as a seasonal spring item on their menus. The Jerusalem artichoke, a native American perennial sunflower, has tubers that look something like a potato, and can be cooked like one or eaten raw in salads. It sells as a specialty vegetable.

Many farmers are amateur mycologists, enjoying the sport of searching the forests for mushrooms that they can add to their dinner pots or sell for extra cash; with some varieties selling at $25 a pound retail, they are likely to find restaurant chefs eager to purchase their wares. Public health departments may regulate the sale of wild mushrooms, however, so be sure to check the legal requirements. Some mushrooms are deadly poisonous, of course, so take the time to consult with experts, study the wild mushrooms available in your area, and harvest only those that are unmistakably safe. Do not forget that even some of the so-called safe mushrooms can cause a reaction in some people, so research carefully to avoid any problems.

Those who have read Gene Stratton Porter's book *The Harvester* know that foragers have been gathering wild herbs for the pharmaceutical trade throughout the twentieth century. The recent accreditation of yew bark as a cancer drug is but one example of natural materials being used for medicines. Ginseng, *Panax quinquefolus,* is a native American herb highly prized by Asian cultures as an aphrodisiac and a cure for everything from impotence to lack of concentration. The Harvester collected wild ginseng and replanted it in his garden in the story Porter wrote in 1911. Today, ginseng continues to be grown and harvested in a number of American states, and farmers selling directly to Asian dealers can make huge profits.

As a wild plant, ginseng grows in cool, shady, hardwood forests that have plenty of acid soil for its roots, taking about eight to ten years to grow to the point where its roots are large enough to harvest and dry. It is quite rare in the wild now, and most of the production is in greenhouses starting from seed. Growers cannot expect to reap the rich rewards of the harvest overnight, but selling to Asian buyers directly can bring in sizable return for the mature root that is cleaned and dried.

Wild herbs are becoming a more important foraging crop for the pharmaceutical industry. Not much material on this subject is yet available, but there will be more every year.

What You Can Plant That Will Go Wild

Foraging can also include cultivating a judicious sampling of trees, shrubs, or plants that will actually "go native." Cherry plum trees become as wild and carefree as any forest tree, and the fruit is very desirable for jams and jellies. Some florists love to get cuttings from the flowering trees early enough in the season to force the blooms in water. Hedgerows of certain varieties of roses become striking trusses of rosehips prized in the city for floral displays, and also coveted in the herb trade.

Certain trees planted in woodlots will be a solid investment, yielding lumbered wood that can be timed to harvest for college tuition fees or retirement plans. Of course, research is important in choosing valued varieties. In the late 1800s, fast-growing eucalyptus trees were imported from Australia to be planted and harvested as timber for an almost instant crop. Unfortunately, the wrong variety was imported, and the wood was useless, cracking and splitting. Their presence all over Northern California is a testimony to hasty research and its discouraging results.

Lilies of the valley naturalize to become to carpets of bloom, and each stem of flowers brings an excellent price in shops. Yarrow grows like a weed, and is considered one in some states; it can be harvested for dried flowers or herbal uses. Daffodils have a hardy reliability that makes them naturalize to bloom in ever expanding pools of color each year. Some of the smaller species of daffodils and tulips grow successfully in mild climates, expanding every year for sales of bulbs, potted plants in bloom, and cut flowers. Many other flowers will grow wild with just a minimum of help from the farmer, and blooms from spring to fall are easily sold in florists' shops, farmers' market stalls, and roadside stands. A grower in San Luis Obispo, California, brings to market her daffodils and branches of quince and almond just forced into bloom to start her selling season. This grower's customers come to her booth first to make sure they can buy and take home with them bouquets of narcissus and daffodils or tall branching stems filled with almond blossoms.

Certain varieties of herbs will grow into small, sturdy shrubs, and once planted, they maintain themselves, allowing the farmer to harvest regularly with a minimum of weeding and care. In the right climates, rosemary will grow like a hedge, and can be sold fresh or used in herbal vinegar. Lemon verbena, renowned as a refreshing lemony herbal tea, grows into small trees whose leaves are easy to harvest. Under certain conditions, mint grows wild and can be harvested all summer long. Nigella, or love-in-a-mist, *Nigella damascena,* self sows and grows like a weed. The seeds of one variety, *N. sativa,* are prized for use in Indian cooking with a flavor similar to cumin. Those seed heads not harvested are coveted by florists for dried arrangements.

FORAGING ON PUBLIC LANDS

Foraging on public lands is called "removing natural resources" and you must have a permit from the managing authority to do so legally. In some cases a fee is charged for each type of material removed, and the amount of material that can be collected is regulated. For example, in California's El Dorado National Forest, your permit to collect seedless pine cones—those cones that have fallen off the trees— will cost $1 for each 100-pound sack, with a $20 minimum. Moss may be collected for $1 per cubic foot, and mistletoe goes for 25 cents per cubic foot. Pine needles sell for $5 a ton. At this national forest, you can purchase a permit that allows collection of more than one item, so for example, your minimum can cover moss and pine cones.

Lest you think the profitability of foraging is overstated, look at the out-of-work loggers in Oregon who forage the woods for pine cones. In some cases, the largest pine cones are selling for as much as 25 cents each. The *Wall Street Journal* reported that Northwest Botanical, an Oregon herb and floral broker, sold ninety-six truckloads of pine cones to Japan in 1991. True, making a living solely from gathering pine cones would be difficult, but the point is that as a part of a plan of year-round diversified production, foraging represents money to be made with a minimum of investment, a point that any savvy Wall Street investment analyst would appreciate.

Each different agency has its own set of rules, and even within agencies, different regions may vary their foraging regulations. Be sure to check with authorities for their procedures and purchase the permit before you begin to load up your truck or car. Foraging on other people's property without permission can land you in jail for trespassing.

As a forager, practice sustainable methods of harvesting to assure a continued crop. Make sure you understand the nature of the plant you are harvesting, and leave enough to grow back the next year.

POSSIBILITIES

Being a successful forager is really a state of mind; you're always checking to see what you have on hand or can make that someone will buy. Here is a sample of a variety of items that you may be able to supply.

Antiques: Old bottles, square nails, canning jars, 1950s kitchen utensils, farming tools and equipment.

Barbed wire: Old varieties are collector's items.

Beekeeping: Beekeepers make money both from renting their hives to orchardists for pollination, and from the sweet harvest of honey, royal jelly, pollen, and wax. Old-fashioned rounds of honeycomb bring premium prices, and homeopathic remedies prescribe comb honey for allergy sufferers.

Berries: Wild berry jams and jellies have been the stuff of roadside stands for years. Chefs order fresh berries for regional dishes. Berries lend themselves to making exotic vinegar, and they are free for the picking.

Burls: In demand by woodcrafters.

Composted manure.

Dried wildflowers for displays: Florists use these all year long.

Edible wild mushrooms, fresh and dried.

Fall foliage for florists.

Firewood: Tree thinnings can be neatly bundled with raffia for kindling starters, or larger logs can be marketed as Yule logs.

Florist materials: Branches with bright fall berries or leaves, plants with seedpods, unusually colored foliage, spring forcing, dried grasses, wheat sheaves.

Fruit tree prunings chipped for smokers, or in neat raffia-wrapped bundles for barbecuing.

Herbal bundles for sweet-smelling firestarters.

Herbs for teas, seasoning blends, wreath materials, potpourri.

Ginseng: Wild and cultivated.

Grasses: Dried for displays.

Greens for wreaths and swags.

Lumber, from old barns and fences, used by decorators.

Mistletoe for Christmas balls or simple sprigs.

Mossy sticks for nurseries and florists.

Orchard wood, for woodcrafters and fine furniture.

Pine cones for wreaths or decorating.

Pine needles for potpourris and crafts.

Potpourris with pine needles, cones, acorn heads, etc.

Rosehips for display and for herbalists.

Sugar maples for winter syrup.

Wildflower seeds, being careful to protect rare plants.

Woodlots.

RESOURCES

Gibbons, Euell. *Stalking the Wild Asparagus.* New York: Van Rees Press, 1962.

The classic book on harvesting edible food from the wild.

McQuarrie, Jack. *Wildcrafting: Harvesting the Wild for a Living.* Santa Barbara, Calif.: Capra Press, 1975.

A bit out of date but useful.

How to Grow Ginseng in Hardwood Forests, Buckhorn Ginseng, Route 4, Richland Center, WI 53581. Contact Ron Dobbs, 608/647-2244.

CHAPTER 5

Selling a Value-Added Product

A nyone with an orchardful of peach trees coming ripe within the same few weeks knows the difficulty of delivering and selling all those peaches while they are in their prime. Regardless of your determined efforts with U-pick sales, restaurant deliveries, farmers' markets, and roadside stands, some of those peaches will get so ripe you'll be forced to dump them, whether into the compost bin or the livestock's dinner pail. There will be culls as well, fruit that is too small to sell or slightly damaged in some way. Making them into value-added products will let you use all your crop and reap the economic reward of a harvest without waste.

Small backyard growers can also take advantage of value-added opportunities. The new techniques of intensive fruit production make even the smallest space an orchard with enough fruit to turn out shelves of jams and jellies. Some of the other products you can make from your vegetables and shrubs can add to the look of your market stall or be lagniappe to thank your best customers. Dried branches of little chilies are favorites for wreath decorations, and, strung like necklaces, smaller chilies delight as kitchen gifts from cookware stores.

Value-added generally means putting the raw fruits or vegetables through an additional process, then packaging and labeling the result. The processed product sells for more money than the raw product. Being able to freeze or dry your harvest for processing later in the season gives you the flexibility to turn out a quality product at your convenience, not nature's. Farmers who make value-added products really appreciate the year-round sales that stabilize the farm's economic base. Security comes with knowing that your preserves, juice, or dried fruits or vegetables are bringing in money long after the trees have been picked clean and the fields are bare.

CHOOSING A PRODUCT

You must come up with the product that suits your style of farming, is unequaled on the marketplace, either in quality or concept, and has some special something the competition does not have. If you merely duplicate what already exists on the shelves with a "me-too" product, the consumer has little incentive to pick it up.

The first rule in creating a successful value-added product is to do your research. Think of yourself as a research technician with a white coat and clipboard, and keep scrupulous figures and records of your costs as you go along. You must devise an item that uses your raw materials efficiently and is uniquely yours. Would the strawberry marmalade you give away at Christmas attract a paying clientele? Would spicy dried tomato jam appeal to adventurous gourmets? Would your customers pay for washed and trimmed broccoli? Your research can be as simple as walking down supermarket aisles looking to see what you can do better, visiting specialty food stores, browsing through farmers' markets, and seeking advice from your friends.

If you decide to make a cooked product, you need to come up with a carefully crafted recipe that uses what you produce with a minimum of store-bought items. If you need to purchase additional items, figure them into the cost of the end product. And be sure to check out wholesale sources; sometimes you'll have to order in advance to assure a supply when you're in the midst of production. If you come up with something absolutely scrumptious but very expensive to make, you may price yourself out of the market. Grammy's treasured family conserve recipe that calls for black walnuts may cost you too much to make. Substituting English walnuts may change the flavor slightly, but it will bring the cost under control.

Get your friends to taste your product and comment critically on it. Do not take the criticism personally; rather, listen closely to their suggestions and make alterations. Ask store owners to sample your product (a good way to get them interested in it from the very beginning). Buy similar items and do taste testings with panels of friends or customers. Continue to experiment until you have come up with something that has the quality you will be proud of and that you can enjoy selling day and night—which is what you will be doing.

Nonfood Products

Of course, value-added products are not just foodstuffs. Guinness McFadden of McFadden Farms in Potter Valley, California, started making garlic wreaths and then California bay leaf wreaths for Williams-Sonoma as a way to keep his farm workers employed year-round. Subsequently, he developed a full line of dried organic herbs he packages under the name of McFadden Farms.

Graham Anderson of Island Sun Greenhouses in Fanny Bay, British Columbia, started creating hanging planters as a sideline to his nursery stock business. He found that people who came to the nursery for six-packs were eager to buy his containers planted and ready to grow. Anderson is able to sell the planted baskets for a great deal more than just his cost for the ingredients, and his repeat clients provide a reliable income every spring. He even has a recycling system, whereby customers returning the containers get a special rate on the new one they take home with them. This marketing technique brings his customers back to him and saves costs on purchasing new containers every year.

A Christmas tree grower in Washington had some requests for container-grown, live Christmas trees. He began to offer them in a number of different sizes. To his surprise and delight, one of his customers called, requesting a live tree for the office. After some experience servicing offices with Christmas trees, the grower came to the happy business of renting live trees to business offices or lobbies. During the first weeks of December, he delivers the trees, and at the end of the month, he picks them up. Even though these trees are not available to sell to his customers during the holiday season, he finds it well worth his while to rent them out, and still have them available the next year for sale or rent. This is a solid example of value-added marketing that pairs a dependable income with an economical use of farm resources.

Value-added can apply to byproducts of meat

production. Wool processed and ready for knitting sells for more than raw fleece. Skins can also be sold successfully. Ostrich growers sell the meat, the skins for leather, and the feathers to the millinery trade. If you add unusual products such as naturally colored fleeces, blue eggs from Araucana chickens, or quail eggs, you can encourage wider market interest. Goat raisers can concentrate on milk, cheese, meat, or leather and fleece, depending on their interests. All of these byproducts are value-added, promising a far better price as a finished product than as raw material. Cashmere fleece from goats is a new farming industry with the potential of returning about $50 a pound for cashmere wool.

GETTING STARTED

Doug Cross and his wife of Canter-Berry Farms in Auburn, Washington, sell to U-pick, deliver to specialty stores and brokers, and freeze enough of their berries to keep up with the steady demand for their jam, thus using all their crop and extending their income throughout the year. Doug figures that for each jar of the farm's blueberry preserves he spends 50 cents on blueberries, 40 cents for sugar, 30 cents for each jar the jam is packed in, 30 cents for labor, and 10 cents for paper and pectin. This jam that costs him roughly $1.16 to make up sells for around $4.

Now if returns like Doug's sound like a great idea to you, first stop and look at your total farm system. Is there really time and staffing to start a whole new sideline? What competition is ahead of you already? Check around to see who else is taking their crop to market in a bottle, jar, or package, and talk to them about what it means to their lives, pro and con. If you decide to pursue a value-added scheme, start with pen and paper and write out a five-year marketing plan that figures your cash flow.

This may sound daunting, but Richard McGuigan of Pippin Ridge Orchard on Denman Island, British Columbia, maintains that he made it past the first rocky years as a processor because he set up a five-year cash flow plan with a generous "screw-up factor." Your plan will look something like this:

	Year	1	2	3	4	5

Costs: Production

permits

material

labor

packaging

labels
  design
  printing

mailing
  postage/insurance
  packaging

Costs: Plant

Rental/upkeep

Utilities

Equipment

Liability insurance

Costs: Marketing

Free samples

Brochures/stationery/
  cards/tee-shirts

Phone

	Year	1	2	3	4	5
Postage for press packets/samples to food writers						
Miscellaneous errors: 15% added to total costs						

Income

Direct sales (farmers' markets, roadside stand, U-pick)						
Specialty outlets						
Mail order						
Distributor						

Make a rough accounting so you have an idea of what you are getting into and whether you can afford it. You are going to balance the happy prospect of economic rewards with the price of your time and labor, plus the costs of equipment, labels, and packaging—which may be as expensive as hand-blown glass jars to ordinary canning jars to cellophane envelopes—and then marketing expenses.

To determine what to charge for your delicious garlic comfit, figure what return on your investment will make this extra work worthwhile for you. For instance, if you want to make an extra $5,000 on value-added products per year, how many units would you have to sell to cover your expenses and make a reasonable profit? Level with yourself and remember that this is *not* the time to be an optimist. Murphy's Law—anything that can go wrong will—should be your constant budget companion.

Once you have looked at the debits, you figure out potential sales. Consider the outlets that might sell your delicious dried fruit packets or pesto. If you have a U-pick stand, farm market, or mail order business, you have a ready outlet for your products. If you sell through someone else, you must expect to pay that person a commission or a consignment fee, which will cut into your profits. If you can deliver your value-added products to specialty grocery stores at the same time as your fresh produce, you will save on delivery costs.

COSTS

On your first run-through, make your cost estimates very generous, and those for income stingy. Again, be sure to add in the hours for labor, because if you get too busy, you'll have to hire someone to keep up production. Try to think of every penny you will need to spend to develop your goods. Crunch the numbers to figure out what the cost of each bottle will be if you make 200 bottles of herb cider vinegar. This price is the unit cost. Usually, the more you make, the cheaper the unit cost because you can begin to buy jars, supplies, and packaging in bulk.

As the five-year-plan list makes clear, there are numerous costs to calculate. One that you may not be aware of is kitchen rental. All food sold to the public must be made in a kitchen certified by the local health department. It may be cheaper to rent than remodel. When scouting to rent a kitchen, remember schools, fairgrounds, churches, and day care centers all have approved kitchens; check out their facilities and see whether the times available to you are convenient and the price is within your budget. Depending on your product, you may have to buy or rent a big freezer. Don't be afraid to buy used kitchen equipment. Many fledgling businesses start out shopping at garage sales or restaurant supply stores to stock up on used equipment without blowing the whole budget.

You will need liability insurance to cover your product, whether it be maple syrup or bay leaf wreaths, so call your insurance agent and find out what it will cost to fully insure your operation; Doug Cross suggests buying as much insurance as you can get.

PREPRODUCTION PREPARATION

There are some important permits and licenses you must have before you go into production. These vary from county to county, state to state, so check with your local health department to find out what you must file before you can start turning out those lovely packets and jars (see Chapter 9 for more on this subject). They will want to know where you are manufacturing and that your facility has been approved for commercial production.

When you are ready to go into production, think carefully about each step to design a process that makes the most efficient use of your produce and your labor. If need be, set up a site plan, sketching out and organizing each step of production. Here is where all the work you did on product development and those notes you carefully kept will come in handy. How many units do you expect to produce each hour, or each shift? How much raw material will you need each shift? If your supplies are at hand in your freezer, you're in luck, but if you're working off the farm, you don't want to drive back to pick up more supplies. Pretty soon, helped by your records, you will know exactly how many lugs of tomatoes, onions, and herbs you need to make the target number of units each shift. Jars and packages will begin to mount up.

LABELING

Your product is going to be sitting on a shelf, and you want the buyer to be drawn to it and lift it into the shopping cart. Who are you, and how does your packaging reflect your business, your philosophy, and your lifestyle? Does a country gingham look match the homemade appeal of your fine cherry-berry jam? Do you want an elegant label reminiscent of a museum-quality botanical drawing to give your gourmet herbal teas an upscale feel? Popcorn labeled with a hard-edged art deco logo may not convey your cozy idea of popcorn shared by a family in front of the fireplace. Linking New World beans with Columbus might antagonize the politically liberal vegetarians you hope to entice with your premium bean mix.

In putting your label together, you will first need to choose a name for your product. You will need to decide what style of artwork will match the product you are selling, and will appeal to the person taking it home. And you will need to write out everything you and the government want on the label to see whether it will fit legibly on the size of label you want.

Pay close attention to what you label your product to highlight its best market advantage. Richard McGuigan found when he called one of his products an apple wine vinegar, his sales dropped immediately. His customers told him they didn't know what apple wine vinegar would taste like. He changed the name back to cider vinegar, and his sales picked up over 500 percent. A strange name will keep your customers from knowing what they are buying, and they want to trust their purchases, so choose your name accordingly.

FDA Requirements

You must also satisfy the requirements of the Food and Drug Administration, so before you start thinking of poetic ways to describe your fabulous fruitie bars, send away for the food labeling guide from the FDA (see Resources at the end of this chapter). The FDA regulates what you can call your product, so you must be sure to follow their guidelines. For example, if you want to use the word *fresh* on your label, your product must never have been heated or frozen, you may use no preservatives, and irradiation at low levels only is allowed. They also have defined terms such as *natural, low, reduced, light, more,* and a host of others. These *descriptors* are carefully set out in their material, and you do not want to design and print your label only to discover you have used a word the FDA forbids.

The government has a few other requirements. On your label must be an ingredients list, with everything that you use in descending order by amount. You must give the weight of the product, the location of its origin, and describe it in ways approved by the FDA. For more details, see page 136.

Bar Codes

When you reach a level of production that allows you to sell to supermarkets or retail outlets that use scanners, you need to consider adding a bar code to your label. These bar codes send a computer message to the cash register that automatically adds the price of the item to the customer's bill and calculates the amount of stock still on the shelf. These are called UPCs, or universal product codes, and are distributed by the Uniform Code Council. The Council will send out an application and a fee schedule upon phone request; see Resources at the end of this chapter. The whole process of receiving a number takes about six weeks.

Designing a Label

Some producers love the challenge of coming up with their own homemade labels. They experiment with potato printing and hand-coloring their logos. At a certain level of production, however, this becomes impossible, and professionally printed labels are a must. Most farmers feel that the money they pay out to commission a professional design for labels is money well spent. Labels can sell their products.

Make sure your label clearly identifies you. Your name should jump off the label. If you have a logo, make sure it is large enough for a customer standing about three feet back from the shelf to see. Besides fulfilling the FDA labeling regulations, plan space for serving suggestions, your address, city, state, and a phone number to call. Many farmers find listing their phone number an excellent way to keep in touch with their consumers, and surprise sales can come from brokers or distributors being able to call easily to inquire about selling your line.

Before you get too far into the process, be sure to register your name and logo to avoid copyright infringement. Although you may be convinced that

Bezongo Beans is such an unusual name no one else has ever thought of it, you may discover that a small jelly bean company in Minnesota had the same brilliant idea, and they registered the name, so they have first right to it. Even if your business is dried tomatoes and you want to share a name with a company that sells register tape, you do not want to waste money in a lawsuit—regardless how silly it seems to you—and you do not want to have to redesign your labels and your marketing strategy.

If you have any room left on the label, you can experiment with text. Celestial Seasonings, the Denver herbal tea company, puts all sorts of ecologically correct sayings on its packages. The labels on Ben and Jerry's ice cream boast clever product names and information about the company. Consumers do appreciate feeling a connection with the manufacturers, and they like to be amused. Coyote Cookhouse Salsa prints the slogan "We make you howl for more" below their logo of a coyote sitting with head thrown back, mouth open. However, these frills must only follow from your sense of the product, and your customer.

You will want to hire a designer to come up with a label that really sells, but there are some guidelines that may help you participate in creating a look you love and can afford. Go out to the market and buy examples of products you think are appealing. Clip advertisements from newspapers and magazines for samples of type, logos, and layouts that you like. Remember, this label will represent you; you must feel good about how your product looks. Your designer will do a better job for you if he or she understands your aesthetics and the quality of your product. If it is a food item, bring the designer a sample, and be sure to show the other products in your line. That experience will assist the designer in coming up with a label that targets the market for you. Interview several designers and ask to see their portfolios. Show them the labels you have collected as examples of the look you like. The designers will show you the kind of work they do, and they should negotiate with you to fit your budget.

When you come up with your final design, use it to identify yourself in all your business transactions. Letterhead, signage, tee-shirts, sandwich boards at your farmers' market booth, and shopping bags should all carry your logo and help you develop an identity for all your products.

In printing, the more labels you print, the cheaper the cost of each individual label. Calculating the number of labels you will need over a period is difficult, but your market plan should give you a guide. You want enough labels on hand so you don't run out, but you don't want so many that you tie up your money in labels for more than a year, and you want the flexibility, at least in the beginning, to change your name or otherwise redo your label if your product isn't selling well.

When the jars start rolling off the production line, you will start to keep accurate records of production, batch numbers, and sales. Producers assign a number to each batch they send out into the world so that if a customer calls to report broken glass in a jar, they can recall all the outstanding jars from that batch. Leave a white box on the label so you can number each successive batch run.

SUPPLIES

You will quickly face the daunting prospect of ordering enough supplies to keep your production line running. Finding you are out of bottles when you have a batch of cider ready is not a happy surprise. But you may not have enough room to store a hundred cases of cider bottles, so you need to consider just where to keep your supplies, from ingredients to mailing materials. Producers buying large quantities negotiate with their suppliers for a yearly contract price and then make arrangements for delivery; sometimes you can secure an agreement that allows you to pay for the year's supply, but take possession just when you need it. Inventory your supplies on hand and keep careful track so that production isn't interrupted.

CO-PACKAGERS

As your business begins to take off, you may reach the point where demand outstrips your ability to meet it. When your product gets to this exciting stage, you will have to set a different course. You may not have the volume of a supermarket item, but if you are finding that your production expenses and your farm schedule are both suffering, you might investigate hiring a co-packager to produce your food items instead of trying to expand on the farm.

Co-packagers offer the services of production facilities and sales reps to assist you with all aspects of product development from start to finish, from creating the concept for you to warehousing the finished product. Their production facilities are fully licensed and inspected. Usually, you work together with them to select a menu of services to fit your situation. In some cases, the co-packager may even buy into the product line and become a partner in the operation. Turning over an amount of control and profit to a stranger has some disadvantages, so evaluate the alternatives to measure what you may gain or lose by taking the production off the farm.

PRICING STRATEGIES

There are no easy formulas to come up with a price that brings you a fair return and sends the product flying out the door. Follow the same procedures as you do for pricing your fresh products. To start, find out what price your competition is selling for. Do you want to meet the competition, overprice it, or underprice it? Some people prefer to start their price high and come down if sales are slow. Others vehemently disagree, preferring to start low and work up to as high as the market will bear. This controversy only points out the necessity of keeping in touch with your buyers. If they pick up your wreath, look at the price, groan, and put it down, it may be priced too expensively. Ask them, right then and there, what they think. Remember, too, that you can charge different prices depending on the location of your market, just as different stores in a chain price by locale. If your sales are slow, try dropping the price and see what happens. If they pick up with the lower price, you know what you need to do. If sales do not increase, you must find out why your product does not interest the passersby. Those endless product surveys you get in the mail or over the phone should notify you that products do not always sell even though they are terrific. Is your labeling off? Are you in the wrong marketplace or do the people who might buy it not know about it? See Chapter 6 for more on marketing.

The satisfaction achieved by those farmers who sell their own value-added products seems to be matched only by their belief in its economic value added to their yearly income. Everyone agrees that the start-up can be expensive, and that pitfalls are many, from running out of jars in the midst of ladling out sticky jam to waking up in the middle of the night realizing you forgot to deliver your cider to the store running a special. Still, there seems to be a quiet pride to the business as well as financial reward.

RESOURCES

Copies of the Food and Drug Administration's Nutrition Labeling and Education Act of 1990 (GPO number 069-001-00045-9) can be ordered from:

Government Printing Office
Superintendent of Documents
710 North Capitol Street NW
Washington, DC 20402

Hall, Stephan F. *From Kitchen & Market: Selling Your Gourmet Food Specialty.* Dover, NH: Upstart Publishing Company, 1992.

A thorough, step-by-step outline of the process of designing and marketing a value-added product.

Uniform Product Code
Uniform Code Council Inc.
7887 Washington Village Drive, Suite 300
Dayton, OH 45459
937/435-3870

CHAPTER 6

From the Farm to the Table: Selling Your Products

Marketing is the bugaboo for all producers. Many producers feel that their job is to create a beautiful or delicious product and someone else should make sure it sells. But successful producers leave nothing to chance, seeing that their apples get to market with the shine still on, or their piccalilli gets prominent shelf space.

A good example of a marketer with tenacity and persistence is Donna Sherrill of Sherrill Orchards in Long Beach, California. She discovered to her horror that her carefully ripened peaches picked up from the farm in pristine condition by the wholesaler were delivered to the terminal market too late for same-day purchase. The buyers from the large stores had already walked through the market and ordered before her fruit was off the truck, and then her fresh-picked fruit sat a whole day or more before the buyers returned. Her tired fruit then competed with newer shipments, and buyers weren't interested.

She remedied the situation by taking turns with her husband delivering to the market by midnight to make sure the buyers saw her fruit first. She then continued to make the rounds of her other outlets not served by her wholesaler, and before leaving town she stopped at the grocery stores to watch her produce arrive. She went to the produce manager, telling him about her fruit and overseeing its placement. Time and time again, she came across instances when her fruit was damaged or overripe from other people's carelessness. She insisted on its removal and a credit to her from her wholesaler. She left her phone number with all the produce managers, and she insisted they call her if they found any problems with her fruit. The managers quickly realized that her standards were the highest, and they would refuse poor-quality fruit, notifying her directly about its condition. Now her wholesaler and her buyers know that she means business, and her professional acumen is respected throughout the region. That definitely is marketing.

In general terms, marketing has two parts: getting your product to where customers will find it, and enticing customers to choose it. There are no simple formulas for marketing, no one approach that will assure success, but learning the basics of marketing can make the difference between a cheese that sells and one that simply sits on the shelf. We all know what happens to cheeses left sitting on the shelf.

A MARKETING PLAN

Even though it may sound onerous and boring, creating a marketing plan is crucial to your success. There are whole volumes written about marketing plans, and flocks of expensive marketing consultants for hire. Anyone with common sense can put together a marketing plan, however. The point of a marketing plan is to lay out a road map you can follow to assure selling your products.

Your plan should have four parts:

1. Grow based on market demand.
2. Grow diversified crops to bring in money all year long.
3. Research outlets for your products.
4. Set measurable sales goals within specified time limits.

Grow Products Based on Market Demand

You may grow fabulous tomatoes, but if you live in a region where every one of your neighbors grows them too, your tomatoes will languish on the market shelves. When thinking about what you want to sell, remember your customer. Figuring out what is in demand is as critical for your crop or product selection as growing conditions and flavor.

Don't forget to analyze byproducts or foraged products that can increase your sales (see Chapter 4). Some of these products you may produce on order for specific clients, such as winter greens to a urban florist, daffodils for drying to a flower stylist, composted poultry manure for an organic products store, or eggs for a local restaurant.

Diversified Crops Bring in
Money All Year Long

Diversifying your crops has a variety of effects on your marketing plan. First of all, it brings you a year-round cash flow, and it allows you to keep in touch with your customers. By keeping in touch with them, you are more likely to keep them as customers. Consider the possibility of value-added products that you can process postharvest or in your slow seasons. Write down all your marketing outlets in a line across a sheet of paper, then list your products underneath them. For example:

	Farmers' markets	Restaurants	Florists	Wholesaler	U-pick
Cole crops	X	X		X	X
Mixed greens	X	X		X	
Sunflowers	X		X		X
Melons	X	X			X
Tomatoes	X	X			X
Dried tomatoes	X	X		X	

Research Outlets for Your Products

Draw up a list of people or places to sell your products. Include the ones you know, but also seek out places you have never approached. Brainstorm with your local farm adviser, family, friends, and business associates. If you have some customers who compliment you on your product, ask them where they shop. They like what they are buying from you and so they will be shopping in places that will also like it.

Don't forget unusual marketing outlets. If you are raising herbs, explore the new-age pharmaceutical industry, which uses tons of herbs. If you are growing unusual vegetables, read the restaurant reviews in the newspaper of the nearest big town to determine which restaurants might want to buy from you.

Jot down all your ideas, clip articles from the newspapers, and start a file of names, addresses, and phone numbers. Remember, you want to create the widest possible base for your sales, both in direct consumer contacts such as farmers' markets, a roadside stand, or delivery to a local grocery store, as well as wholesalers. The direct sales outlets bring you the greatest return, because you are not paying a commission to someone for helping you sell. However, you may not be able to sell a big crop on your own when it all comes ripe at about the same time. Therefore, if you have volume sales you should also line up some indirect sales outlets.

Measurable Goals within Specified Time Limits

Everyone needs incentives; the old carrot-in-front-of-the-horse concept is a sound and recommended business practice. Set goals for yourself, but make them specific, not vague and unmanageable. The starting place for your goals is your cash flow projections. If you want to bring in $15,000 from your produce from April to October, take the time to look at each crop you are growing, estimate what your yields may be, and calculate what the sales will total.

Be realistic about your goals. If you set impossible goals, you will discourage both yourself and your staff. Once you have a clear month-by-month projection, take the time to discuss the plan with all of your team. Make sure everyone understands and agrees. You may have to make adjustments if everyone thinks your goals are impossible. If you exceed the monthly goal, great; if you fall below, look at the reasons why. Did you overestimate, or did sales fall? If the latter, try to determine the cause. Setting goals will give you the confidence and sense of control over your business that will help you to succeed.

PICKING UP NEW CUSTOMERS

Next, begin contacting your file of prospects. This "cold calling" can be managed in a variety of ways. Unless you have a personal contact with a potential new client, a letter followed up with a phone call is best. Remember, there are preferred times of day to call people depending on their business. Chefs can't come to the phone during mealtimes, many vegetable distributors are gone after 2 P.M., and some grocery store buyers are too busy placing orders at 8 A.M. to talk with you.

Cold calling is an art, and like an art, it will improve with practice. Rehearse first with the phone still on the hook. First, identify the person you want to contact. If secretaries will not put you through to the people you want, "chat up" the secretaries. They can be very helpful in steering you to the right people in the company, letting you know the best time to contact them, and telling you whether you have targeted that company's needs.

When you reach the person you want to sell to, let him or her know clearly what your product is, how much you can deliver, and for how long. If the company cannot use your product at the moment, be sure to let them know you have a quality item and would like to keep in touch. The company will have a number of growers selling to them already, but if you keep coming back, they will look for a way to work you in.

If anyone offers you a deal that confuses you, or the price seems too low, remember, you can always take time to consider the offer. Let the person know you appreciate the offer, and take time to look at your figures to see how it will affect you, and even come up with a counteroffer. "Thank you for making the offer. I would like very much to have you as a client, but I need time to look at the figures to see whether that will work for me" is a phrase that gives you some flexibility. Be sure to end the conversation with a telephone appointment later that day or the next day to finalize the offer.

MARKETING BY MEETING THE NEEDS OF YOUR CUSTOMERS

A very important part of marketing is word-of-mouth advertising, which is, in fact, your best advertising. Your reputation is the most valuable marketing tool you have. If you are known as an enterprising supplier who delivers what is promised, customers will seek you out. First of all, your product needs to be of the highest quality. If you can come up with the quality, you will come up with customers. Burtis Jansen of Colusa Cold Storage in Colusa, California, figures he sells only 40 percent of his crop, because that 40 percent is the very best he can grow. Dorothy Coil, a grower in Lodi, California, personally handpicks everything from her two-acre garden that she sells because she wants to be known for the perfection of her vegetables. She says no one else seems to know how to pick and pack squash blossoms without tearing the petals.

Service and dependability are two parts of your marketing plan that should never be forgotten. Snagging a new customer is hard work, so take good care of your customers to keep them. You may be used to pumping your own gas at the gas station now, but if you had a choice, you'd certainly like someone to wash your windows and fill the tank. Service is making sure your customers are happy with your products. Ask them not once but regularly whether they are pleased with what you sell them. Call them separately from taking orders and tell them that you value their trade, and you are doing a survey to make sure they are satisfied. Most people hate to be critical, and many of us will just quietly drift away if we get a box of cucumbers that are too old, or become vaguely discontented because the delivery time is later than we need.

Dependability is the other factor that makes a grower's reputation. Suppose you have a deal to deliver two boxes of blood oranges to a chef who has planned a special dessert all printed up on the menu. If you don't show, you'll have to find another chef to sell to. Your customers have their reputations on the line, and they are trusting you to hold up your end of the bargain, so they can deliver on theirs. Although no one talks about it openly, trust really is the basis of business. Keeping your customers happy will keep your customers.

There are times when the truck breaks down or the crop fails, and almost everyone is understanding about the occasional mishap. But if you anticipate a problem with delivering on your contracts, do not wait till the last minute to let your buyers know. Call immediately. It may be a tough call, but if you give them time to make other arrangements, they will thank you for it. And if you can make the arrangements for them, they will be even more grateful. So if you cannot come through with the boxes of miniature corn, and you know someone who can, set up the substitution and offer that to your customer. They will remember you tried to help, not that you left them in the lurch.

A much overlooked part of marketing is your staff. No matter how large or small the number of your employees, think of them as an investment you make in your business. They are just as important as the seeds you plant, because they represent you as much as your product. A grumpy employee will chase away customers. We have all had the experience of stalking out of a store and vowing never to go back because of the way we were treated. Employees who like their jobs and who know what they are selling will double or triple your sales. The time you take to train them is really money in the bank. Your customers will look forward to cheery exchanges with staff they get to know over the season. Good salespeople are those who have cottoned on to the secret that selling the product is more than trading goods for money.

PUBLICITY AND ADVERTISING

It is a sad lesson indeed to have answered the challenge of getting your unusual melons into the stores only to have them sit there unnoticed. If you are growing unusual products, you will need to help educate your customers and create the demand that means customers begin to seek out your products.

Get to know your local food columnist. Journalists have to come up with stories every week, and you would be surprised to know how grateful they are when someone calls up and gives them a story. If you have some new product, or a particularly interesting story about your farm, sit down and write it up. If that seems too daunting, call the columnist and tell him or her about it. Offer samples, recipes, a tour of the farm; send photographs of products growing in the fields. If local restaurants are featuring your produce, mentioning that fact will please your chef customers. Continue to stay in touch with your columnist. If something appears in print, have it laminated and display it everywhere you can.

Adopting a high profile in your community will attract attention to your farm. Join the Chamber of Commerce and offer produce for special events in exchange for a mention in the program. Participate in local festivals and donate products for charity raffles. When people see your name in print and hear it mentioned different places, they will look for your products to take home.

For some companies, advertising may mean purchasing time during the Super Bowl, but for you, advertising can be as simple as a small notice in the newspaper that your extra-special seedless yellow watermelon will be for sale at the local farmers' market. Paid advertising can be very expensive, so look for alternatives. Recipes and printed information at the point of purchase can really make a difference in sales.

Offer to go to your specialty grocery store and do a varietal tasting of your produce for the salespeople. Teach them how to tell when the produce is ripe and how to handle the more perishable varieties. Take time to work with the consumers. Often the stores will welcome you to spend an afternoon or a Saturday morning teaching their customers about your products, and they will often run a special on your produce during that time.

FARMERS' MARKETS

Certified farmers' markets are one of the most profitable ways to sell your product, because you exchange money directly with the consumer. Market fees are minimal, and you do not have to spend the time and money to grade and package your produce.

There are restrictions, notably that you may sell only the produce you yourself grow, and the product must be of premium quality. Market days provide the opportunity to socialize with your customers and work on educating them about your products. The market crowds are friendly and interested in your products, exclaiming over the size and flavor. Although the hours are long, your rewards come with the brisk sales of your products and the pleasure in having customers becoming friends you look forward to seeing every week.

All farmers' markets are regulated. Usually there will be a market manager to help you with the regulations so you can become a certified seller. You will need to fill out forms to register and provide certification if you are an organic grower. Because the markets try to offer a cross-section of products, you will be asked to register yours, whether they be jams and jellies or eggs and potatoes.

Different markets are open at different times, and if you live in an area that has several markets, you may be able to sell more than once a week. If you have choices, spend time researching which market offers the best chance of selling your products. A grower in Modesto, California, chooses to drive eighty miles to Bay Area farmers' markets because she can get twice as much for her tomatoes from those suburbanites as her neighbors would pay. Be sure to take the time to visit the farmers' markets in your area to see what is being sold and, equally important, who is buying it. Some markets may specialize in ethnic produce; others may have more value-added products. Try to anticipate how your products would fit into each market. You can adjust your crops through planning to attract the kinds of customers who come to the market. You may even find that your customers will ask you to grow a certain crop for them.

If you have choices, take time to get to know how the market manager works with the growers and the consumers who come to the market. A supportive market management will stage festivals and events to draw crowds into the market. Lynn Bagley of the Marin Farmers' Market sends out mailings to thousands of Bay Area residents about varietal crop tastings, farm days, country festivals, and fruit pie contests. Her farm days feature live animals, agricultural groups, lots of show and tell. Busloads of children, their parents, and seniors all arrive to enjoy the day. If you have an active manager, you will be assured of having waves of customers and selling out most days.

Before choosing your market, factor in other ways to make your trip to town the most efficient use of your time and money. Can you set up appointments to deliver to a specialty grocery store, or bring in dried materials for florists? Is it possible to drop off cases of fresh squash to a restaurant customer before setting up at the market? The more sales outlets you cover in a single trip, the more cost-effective that trip is.

When your spinach is ready for harvest, the spinach of other sellers will be ready too, and the prices will drop. Think about how you can sell your produce differently. If you have the earliest ripe tomatoes, customers will flock to your booth. Look at all the cycles of your harvest. Your squash plants have flowers you can sell, or you might try to sell baby squash as well as the more mature squash.

Educating the Customer

Consumers who understand the value of the food they buy from you will return again and again.

Teach them about different varieties of produce and explain how the flavor is affected by conditions of climate and soil. Help them get a sense of you as a farmer, and your farm as a way of life. Check cookbooks out from the library or ask your restaurant clients for special ways to cook your products. Print up some recipes so your customers will know what to do with any unusual vegetables. If they buy something new to them and let it rot in the refrigerator, they will not come back to buy other things.

Offering samples is a very effective sales technique, but the practice is decried as unsanitary by many public health departments. Ask your manager what regulations govern your market. If you are allowed to provide samples, bring sanitary cutting boards and knives, and offer everyone a bite of your vegetables or fruit. Not only will they stop, but they will take the time while they munch to look at what else you have in your booth. Eating is believing, and your sales will reflect the effect of your produce on your customers' taste buds.

Planning Your Booth

If you have a flair for the artistic, decorate your booth so it will stand out. Return buyers will be looking for you, and you can jog their memories with your booth. If you have a logo, be sure to display it to its best advantage. Some farmers have tee-shirts printed with their logo that they and all their staff wear to help identify them. One seller in San Luis Obispo, California, says that her most effective marketing dollars were spent on a brightly colored cloth she spreads over her table, and wide, woven willow baskets in which she arranges her wares. The arrangement of the produce seems to call people in to buy.

There are some disadvantages to selling in a

farmers' market, and you should be prepared to deal with them. If the market stalls are not under cover, bad weather will keep customers away. The market management may prohibit you from selling all your crops so they can achieve diversity in the market, and you may have to pay a small certification fee for those you do sell. The hours can be very long by the time you add in picking, traveling, setup, selling, take-down, and the trip home. There is competition between sellers in the market, and sometimes squabbling as well. Still, good farmers' markets are much beloved by farmers because good managers try to keep their farmers happy and the customers coming back week after week by negotiating with the agricultural commissioners and the health department, and by organizing festivals and special events.

U-PICK

U-pick operations are another way to set up a direct market outlet, with the advantages of staying close to your fields and orchards. Running a stand on your property means you can harvest your produce just before the stand opens for optimal freshness, and pick only as much as you need for display, bringing in more from the fields when necessary, thus avoiding waste. You can set your own prices and you get the cash from your sales immediately.

If you want to run a U-pick, your location is an important predictor of your success. Most U-picks are within fifty miles of a large urban area. Those farther out have worked to design their farm as a family destination with daylong activities, such as hay bale mazes, a farm education center, farm tours, hayrides, and festivals. One farmer has alfalfa dispensers for his petting zoo, and with a chuckle, he admits that $1.25 worth of pellets brings him $70 from the dispenser, and that the kids love to feed his animals, who get fat and happy.

Many U-picks specialize, harvesting just one crop, such as blueberries or apples, but other farmers find a diversified production system that brings in a succession of crops over the summer months when city people plan pleasant country trips is worthwhile. An extended season of crops brings customers back again and again, providing a base of sales that makes the long hours worthwhile.

You need to realistically examine some of the difficulties of operating a U-pick business. Your staff and family must agree with you that a U-pick will be a benefit, because their cooperation is crucial. Some people feel invaded when strangers show up on their doorstep. Once the warm weather arrives and the harvest begins, your stand needs to be open seven days a week. And don't forget, it will take a while to get your business established, and you may not see a profit for several years or until you have developed a group of customers who make your stand a regular stop.

Planning will help you anticipate problems, and many farmers, once they have negotiated the hurdles, have a great time opening their fields and orchards to the public. They find it entertaining to run an operation where people come out and do all the work of picking plus pay for the privilege. While they have folks on their land, they use the opportunity to market a variety of their other crops, from seasonal produce to farm gifts and value-added products. Some U-picks with limited crops work to extend the season with value-added products, nursery starts, dried beans, and frozen and dried fruits. There is even the option of purchasing a re-sale license and selling produce for your neighbors.

Because crops come in at the same time, having the public picking for you can help you complete your harvest. Some farmers, however, do not want strangers in their fields, particularly strangers who don't have a clue as to how to harvest the produce without damaging the plant or tree. They cite trampled rows, fruit half eaten and thrown away—in short, waste. Nita Gizdich of Gizdich Ranch in Watsonville, California, agrees that there is some waste, but her staff are carefully trained to meet all customers and individually show them how to harvest. Even if the picker says he or she is experienced, the staff in a friendly but firm manner state that they will just quickly go over the best way to pick that protects the plant.

Regulations

You will want to check with the local farm agent and zoning board about any county requirements for running a commercial operation on a farm. Zoning requirements may include parking lots and bathroom facilities. You'll also be subject to a variety of health, police, and fire regulations. The agricultural commissioner will pay you a visit to certify you, and in some cases will charge for the certification. You may also encounter zoning restrictions when you want to put up signs to direct people to your farm (see "Signage," page 93). If you are building a market, there will be building permits required.

Insurance

Customers overreaching for that perfect apple on top of a tree are a hazard. (Many U-pick fruit tree operations cultivate dwarf varieties to eliminate the use of ladders, a sensible precaution.) Call your agent and purchase as much liability insurance as you can, to cover every possible problem. If you have an accident of any type, whether involving customers and their cars or a personal injury, sit down and write out a complete report of the incident and file it immediately with the police and your insurance agent. Some U-picks will tell you they have never had problems. Those who were taken to court are not in business any longer to relate their stories.

Handling Cash

Make sure the money you take in stays with you, because U-picks can be vulnerable to vandalism and theft. Teach your cashiers the habit of leaving the customer's cash out while making change until the transaction is completed. Keep all money in a cashier's box or cash register. Have someone *always* standing next to it. Empty the box throughout the day, leaving only about $20 in change in the box at any one time.

On the other hand, consider Adams Station Produce, in Gasquet, California. They run a very basic sales organization, picking and displaying their produce, and have wrestled with the problems and distractions of waiting on their customers instead of working on the weeds in the tomato beds. They decided to operate on the honor system, with a saucer and $5 in change, and they have had no problems. They do emphasize that it is their location and the good will of the community that make this work; still, they keep notes sent by visitors from all over the nation who were thrilled to find prize-winning tomatoes, as well as simple trust, on display.

Parking

Taking good farmland out of production to provide for cars seems a terrible waste, but your customers will expect convenient parking, and will not come back if they have to traipse through mud or dust, or hike long distances to get to the picking area. Take time to plan out the location of your lot, and consider "hayrides" if your fields are too far from the parking lots. Setting up satellite parking lots close to the picking areas is sometimes a possibility. Consider gravel or paving if your parking lot is a summertime dust field and a wintertime mudhole. Have separate entrance and exits, and be sure to mark them clearly. Be sure to locate your checkout stand near the parking lot so you can oversee everyone's departure and collect their money.

Restrooms

If you want large groups of people to come, clean, well-appointed restrooms are essential. Depending on how you are setting up your operation, from picking apricots once a year to a year-round scheme with festivals and bus tours, your bathrooms can be portapotties or cement floor facilities. In some cases, you may want portapotties near the picking area, and fancier ones near the main farm store. Zoning regulations designate certain restrictions, and your own water and septic systems will establish others. Certainly, common sense dictates that you start small, with room to expand as business increases.

Having good restrooms opens up a number of opportunities you would otherwise miss. You may be able to encourage your local tourist board to work with major tour companies to lead spring blossom tours for seniors or international visitors. At the very least, your market could be a rest stop for travelers who want fresh fruit to nibble on the road, a chance to stretch their legs, and a clean bathroom to use before the next stop two hundred miles down the road.

If you are located in a heat belt, make some provision for the comfort of your visitors. Water for thirsty children and adults is very important, as is shade. Of course, you have a great opportunity to sell ice-cold carbonated drinks, adding to your daily take, and you can consider further embellishments as your trade grows.

Advertising and Promoting Your U-Pick

Even if you have the most luscious strawberries in the county, if you do not advertise, you may not get any customers, and the ones who do stumble in may never find you again. Make out a plan of all the ways you can reach people. Consider both paid and free publicity when you draw up your campaign. Classified ads in the newspapers of large towns always bring people in. A brochure in local stores and motels may help you catch the eye of people just passing through.

Press releases.   Food editors might like to visit and write up your farm, so consider putting together a packet of information about your farm, your crops, and family recipes. Travel editors might be interested in doing an article on farm trails—suggested routes for city people to purchase farm products in the country—so send a similar packet to them. You can start things off by sending out press releases. These are very simple to prepare; here is what one looks like.

FOR IMMEDIATE RELEASE

What: The first peaches of the season
Where: Johnson's U-Pick Fruit Stand, 3300 Old
   River Road, Lincoln, Iowa
When: Open 8am to 6pm

Tim and Terry Johnson are proud to announce the 10th season of U-pick peaches at their Heritage Ranch. The earliest, freshest peaches are just ready for the picking on trees small enough for everyone to reach. Old folks and young folks can come to the ranch to pick, picnic at the tables under the trees, feed the baby pigs and lambs, and take home other produce fresh from the large home garden Tim and Terry run. On the next four weekends, folks who purchase ten pounds of fruit will take home a free pie.

Call 332-4500 for directions or schedules of other fruits coming into season.

Contact Tim or Terry Johnson, Heritage Ranch, 3300 Old River Road, Lincoln, Iowa.
Phone: 332-4500

Farm trails. Many farmers have worked with their local tourist boards or extension advisers to set up farm trail organizations. Farmers who are open to visitors for U-pick or on-site sales publish their names, farms, crops, and hours together in a brochure. This cooperative effort can be organized as a nonprofit or as a volunteer committee to oversee the farm trail members. You share costs of advertising, publishing, and marketing. Across the country, farm trails are bringing customers to farms with great success.

Signage. Signs for U-picks are essential to help your customers find you. If your signs are on private property, usually you won't run into any regulating agencies. If you want roadside signs along county land or right-of-way, however, your local zoning ordinances may designate a total of square footage allowed. Farmers find it effective to mount large signs near the major highways, with smaller signs along the way to lead cars to the farm. Signs with your logo help identify you clearly. Designing your major signs so you can hang on extra signs as crops come available alerts your customers when their favorite crops are ripe. Many farmers give out cards with the farm name and phone number on one side and a map to the property on the other.

MAIL ORDER

Mail order is another form of direct marketing, because you sell the product directly to your customers. Mail order can be particularly effective for value-added products, products that have a seasonal theme, unusual or premium fruits, or products that may be especially attractive as gifts. Mail order has expenses attached to it, however. You have to plan on costs for designing and mailing a brochure as well as purchasing packaging supplies and postage. Some of these costs you will pass on to your customers in the form of a handling fee, but the others are cash outlays to figure into the price of your product.

At the center of a mail order program is the mailing list. Mailing lists are time-consuming to create and maintain, but the rewards of a good list are certain. The primary rule of mail order is to collect names of your customers at every opportunity. If you have a U-pick business, be sure to place a mail order sign-up sheet right next to the checkout stand. A list at your farmers' market stall can offer to mail products to shut-ins, to friends for an occasion, or as a surprise gift.

Most mail order veterans expect a one in ten return on their mailings, and they are very careful to weed through their lists to delete people who have not responded to a mailing over the course of one year. Sometimes businesses enclose a mail card to be mailed back if the customer wishes to stay on the mailing list. Make sure you update your list regularly.

Quick turnaround is very important for most customers. Your service is crucial to attract the repeat customers who make mail order a steady business. Prompt fulfillment establishes an image of competence and efficiency for you and your business, and that image reflects on your product. Special touches help to create a relationship with your customer. A card containing farm news or a note on the invoice thanking them for the order makes customers feel they have gotten a perk with their product.

If you have seasonal mail order products, such as wreaths for Christmas, take note of when other mail order companies begin to send out catalogs, and don't get left behind. If you are mailing catalogs just once a year, a postcard can remind your customers that you are waiting for their orders and to call if they have questions.

Be prepared to spend time on the phone with your mail order customers. They will call wanting to know whether the berry jam is tart or sweet, or whether it has skins in it or is jelly, no matter what you have clearly stated in the catalog. Taking the time to talk over the phone when you have an orchard to pick can be difficult, but phone work is an essential part of the business, so figure out how to manage it. Some small mail order companies use their answering machines, and leave a friendly message about being out herding the sheep and promising to call back.

SELLING TO RESTAURANTS

For many growers, chefs are their favorite customers. Chefs work with food all day long, and they know and appreciate fresh, quality produce when they see it. Farmers find they are welcomed and peppered with questions about the different fruits and vegetables they provide, and often even given a snack for the road. Chefs also follow food trends closely, so they have exciting new ideas about crops you might plant, assisting you with staying abreast of the specialty food market. You may find, however, that the small volume chefs order makes the time to pick for and deliver to them less cost effective than other sales outlets (they may request delivery two or three times a week), so crunch your figures carefully.

Chefs have rigid schedules, so they expect their suppliers to deliver their orders on time and up to standard. Communicating with chefs is critical for a successful business relationship. A grower who discovers that rabbits got into the carrots, or the lettuce was bruised in the hailstorm, had better call the chef immediately to give fair warning. Rich Collins of California Vegetable Specialties uses as his motto "Surprises are for birthday parties" to remind himself to keep in touch with his customers.

Talk to your chef customers before you finalize your planting plan to find out what the restaurants want like to serve, and what quantities they would like you to deliver. Think carefully about what varieties to choose when you plant, and try to present crops the restaurants can use. If one of your chefs loves sugar snap peas all spring long, you will want to choose varieties to stretch the season as much as you can. If your Italian restaurant cooks fresh marinara sauce, you can plant early-, mid-, and late-season sauce tomatoes to keep them happy. Knowing what they want will help you plan your harvest yields the most effectively.

Check when your chef would prefer you to bring in your order, and be sure to be on time. Stay away during lunch and dinner hours. Kitchens are kept clean, so don't walk in with muddy boots and plunk down a box of tomatoes covered with oozy clay. Your chef may invite you to sit down and have a cup of coffee, but if the bread did not rise and the potatoes burned, then your chef is busy and only wants to nod hello. Be sensitive to the kitchen routine, and drop off your produce with a friendly wave if it feels like everyone is behind schedule.

Chefs are budget-conscious, so they will expect to pay market prices. Bring your price list with you. They do appreciate fine quality, but they have worked out their menus according to ingredient prices and the amount they can charge for the dish. Most chefs can tell you exactly how much each dish they prepare costs. If you have small quantities of a special fruit or vegetable, ask them if they might use it. Also, if you have some seconds, offer them at a reduced rate. Chefs are frugal and inventive, and they can take a lug of slightly off peaches and make a superb peach sauce.

Payment, as with all your customers, is clearly specified when you take the order. Work out the terms of payment and deliver an invoice with your products. Many restaurants will ask for credit, but farmers have found that the restaurant business is very volatile, and too many requests for credit may indicate a restaurant in trouble. Payment should be at least once a month; every two weeks is a better schedule.

SELLING TO WHOLESALERS

A number of channels of distribution are available to the grower who produces too much volume to sell through direct markets. You have only so many hours in a day, and you can satisfy only so many customers. If you find you have more cucumbers bursting out on your vines than you are able to sell yourself, then think about selling to a wholesaler.

Wholesalers come in many different guises, from shippers to brokers to distributors. Before you join forces with a wholesaler, do your research. Ask other growers what their wholesaler's record is like. Plan on interviewing wholesalers just as you would check around for the best dentist or doctor; after all, these people will be directly responsible for your economic health, and you need to work with someone you trust. *The Blue Book* and *The Red Book* (see Resources at the end of the chapter) both give credit ratings for wholesalers. Make an appointment with a buyer to find out what their terms are and to see for yourself what kind of operation they run. They may not have a great deal of time to give you, but meet them and take a tour of their facility.

The wholesalers will already be working with a number of growers, and they may not need your products when you first talk to them. Be persistent, and if you decide they are the company you want, continue to call them. Some companies will expect large volume, others will call you for a couple of cases. Check what their sales terms are, and how they expect delivery. If you have enough volume, some companies will schedule a regular pickup; others want you to ship. Brokers have you ship directly to the customer.

Wholesalers increase the sales you can achieve, and they do the accounting, invoicing, and collecting for you. If you are losing money because you are hopeless at setting prices and doing paperwork, a wholesaler, even with their commission, may save you money. You will need to work with your wholesaler as intensively as you work with your other customers to make sure both of you are happy with the business arrangements. Communication is essential, because the wholesaler sells to his customers on the basis of what you have estimated your yield to be. If a freeze stunts your bean harvest, let the wholesaler know immediately. If wet weather wipes out your strawberries, make the phone call.

RESOURCES

California Department of Food and Agriculture, *How to Establish and Operate a Roadside Stand.* Distributed by the Small Farm Center, University of California, Davis.

Whateley, Booker T. *How to Make $100,000 Farming 25 Acres.* Emmaus, Pa.: Rodale Press, 1987.

Subscription Services

The following two books are actually subscription services offering a variety of different products. They are the best way to check on the reliability and economic viability of the wholesalers you want to sell your produce to. They are very expensive, and because the material is copyrighted, they are not in libraries. The information is excellent.

The Blue Book
Fruit and Vegetable Credit and Marketing Service
Produce Reporter Company
315 West Wesley Street
Wheaton, IL 60187
630/668-3500

Two semiannual books, phone assistance, business
reference; $435 annually.

The Red Book Credit Services
10901 West 84 Terrace
Lenexa, KS 66214
800/252-1925
www.rbcs.com

A variety of special services, such as updated ratings,
a weekly newsletter, a CD Rom, and a produce industry
handbook; $510 annually.

CHAPTER 7

Country to City Connections

Because of the difference in living styles between the country and the city, a whole new learning field has grown up called *agricultural literacy*. Those dedicated to developing its policy, strategies, and curriculum feel that this knowledge will help sustain and support small farmers in America today. A very simplified version of their argument states that people living in cities will appreciate farmers and the food they produce if they understand the steps involved in bringing a fresh carrot from the earth to the table. Understanding and appreciating the products of the farm will encourage everyone to eat more carefully, and by seeking higher standards of food quality, consumers will be willing to pay higher prices for better-tasting and more wholesome food. Eating wholesome food will improve the health of the society and safeguard the future of its children.

An example that demonstrates the importance of this relationship between consumer and farmer can be found in France. There, the farmers' markets showcase an incredible diversity of agricultural products, from cheese to currants to small, very perishable *fraises du bois* eagerly purchased as soon as they appear in early summer. French shoppers seek out the finest and freshest produce in bustling streetside markets in Tours and Lyons, stalls and carts in country towns. Market days are eagerly awaited events in every region, so much so that food writer Patricia Wells in her *Eating in France* makes a careful note for travelers of the time and place of market days all over France. In Paris, Fauchon displays finger-size carrots, cherries the size of currants, and lime green lettuces as carefully as Tiffany's displays diamonds.

You who are participating in this growing American movement can make a profit while helping the cause of agriculture in America. Agritourism is emerging as a new rural industry. The term loosely covers a number of possibilities that bring city people into the country, and the pleasure of the exchange between two different lifestyles is as transporting as jetting to a far-distant destination. It reflects both a current trend to sentimentalize the country and urbanites' deeply felt need to reconnect with nature. City people who grew up on family farms remember their childhoods fondly. The smell of new-mown hay, the sound of chickens cackling, and the sight of cows grazing in a green pasture bring back pleasant memories for them, and create enjoyable new experiences for lifelong city dwellers. These bucolic images are scenes that occur every day on farms throughout America. City families can plan a vacation on a farm, working or simply enjoying walks down quiet country lanes. Agritourism helps the cause of agricultural literacy because when you have slept under a farm roof and woken to help harvest the apples, you never eat an apple the same way again. For a city person, a petting zoo, the chance to help herd the sheep, cross-country skiing over country hills, or camping next to a stream on a farm are unforgettable opportunities to savor the splendor of the country.

BED AND BREAKFAST FARMS

If you have a sociable temperament, like to cook, and have extra rooms in your farmhouse, running a bed and breakfast can be a stimulating and rewarding way to bring in extra cash. To be successful, however, follow the rule guiding most businesses: "Location, location, location." In order to fill the beds, your farm must be close to a city, recreational area, or travel route. If people pass through or visit your area, you will attract paying visitors. Those who live in snowy winter conditions will find that buying the equipment to create cross-country trails will turn your bed and breakfast into a winter recreational area. Winter stays at your farm for skiing can be day only or overnight. An out-of-the-way scenic spot will be attractive to your guests, but it will require extra marketing effort.

Regulations

Before you start counting your sheets, make a visit to your local planning department to check on zoning regulations; they are different in every county. Just because your friend runs a B and B in the next county does not mean you can go into business the same way. If you are using only one or two rooms, you may not need a code kitchen or second-story emergency exits. Check about licensing requirements. There are bed and breakfast associations in almost every state, and they can be invaluable in helping you get started.

Barbara Hussey of MeadowView Country Gardens in Grants Pass, Oregon, gives out sage advice to those starting the permit process. If you receive a no for an answer, smile pleasantly, ask to see the regulations, then go home and do your homework. Talk to your neighbors and get their support. Talk to your farm adviser, county board of supervisors—in short, lobby everyone you can think of, and ask for their help in interpreting the codes favorably for you. Barbara worked for one year to get full permission for her farm restaurant with beautiful gardens. She says that persistence coupled with a cheerful, friendly manner carried her through a thicket of bureaucratic obstacles.

Learn about the zoning differences between exclusive farm use and commercial. Barbara found that keeping her farm as exclusive farm use had long-term advantages a commercial zoning lacked. Get a number of opinions about zoning changes before you make any. These changes also have tax ramifications. If you need to remodel to accommodate your guests, check the tax regulations to determine tax-deductible expenses.

Precautions

One of the primary rules a country host must remember is that the guests may never have visited a farm before, so take precautions. Children think all four-legged animals like to be hugged, petted, or ridden, and city kids have no sense of the danger. Their parents may only have seen goats in a zoo, and have no idea that even the gentlest goat trying to get a handful of grass can knock over a small child. Make sure all your animals are fenced in and post clear warning signs. If your goat tends to butt, make sure a sign on his pen warns to stay out of Billy's pasture. Some ducks and geese will hiss and attack legs, so pen these animals out of the main area where guests come and go. But gentle animals bring great pleasure to city guests, so when possible, share them with your guests.

No precautions are perfect, so you must have an insurance policy that provides full liability coverage. Be sure to consult with your agent before you start your business.

The Amenities

Your guests expect a professional innkeeper, no matter how few rooms you have. You'll want to provide all the basic amenities of a Holiday Inn: bedside lighting, smoke alarms, well-lit hallways, clean bathrooms. Good beds are a must, and for optimum flexibility most innkeepers have at least one bedroom with a queen-size bed and another with two singles. Remember, the singles can be fastened together to make a king-size bed.

Guests expect a lavish, farm-fresh breakfast, usually starting with a course of fruit, and then pancakes, French toast, waffles, or eggs. But many visitors have dietary restrictions; ask about special diets when taking reservations. Piping hot coffee first thing in the morning is a necessity, but always prepare for those who prefer herbal or black tea. Evelyn Sonka of Sonka's Sheep Station Inn of Myrtle Creek, Oregon, says that although her guests may be watching their weight, they always make an exception for their farm stay, so be sure to have enough food. She tells the guests when breakfast will be served, and she and her husband sit down and eat with them.

Evelyn loves the business because she can take reservations only when she wants. Her business is strictly reservation-only so when she wants to be away, she simply tells callers she is full for that day. She keeps a guest book and tries to stay in touch with her guests. She has found that there are a lot of downtown Victorians, but not a lot of working farms offering bed and breakfast. She regularly prints a brochure and stays in all the guidebooks.

Publicity

Brochures are one of the best ways to let tourists know about your brand of country hospitality. Full-color brochures can be very expensive, so start with a simple brochure that uses attractive paper and a different color of ink. Unless you have writing and design skills, find someone who will create the brochure with you. (Don't forget the possibility of trading a weekend at your bed and breakfast for their work.) Be sure to include all your rules: no smoking, no arrivals after 11 P.M.; open only on weekends, whatever. When your brochure is printed, send it to the local board of tourism, and have it displayed at local markets. Send brochures with a letter to the travel editors of newspapers in the largest cities near you. They may file it for a roundup article at a later time.

CORPORATE PICNICS
AND PRIVATE PARTIES

Corporations and businesses are always looking for unusual sites for company picnics and celebrations. If your farm has picnic facilities, including parking areas, picnic benches, toilets, and an outdoor area with running water for food service, you may be able to rent out part of your farm by the day. There are risks involved such as plugged-up plumbing, allergic reactions to bee stings, and supervisory time, but if you run a U-pick operation you may be quite accustomed to handling crowds and able to cope with all their needs. Working with the public can be a superb marketing opportunity to win new customers who will return to your business time and time again.

If there are local educational agencies involved in creating city-to-country links in your area, you'll want to coordinate with them, because they have many contacts and have the credibility to introduce you to larger companies. Work with local tourist boards and nonprofit agricultural groups active in agricultural literacy projects.

Be sure to photograph each group that comes to your property. Inexpensive snapshots have two great marketing functions. First, they allow you to keep contact with the group pictured. Reminder photos sent out about six months after the event help revive the pleasant memories of your location at a time when next year's event is being planned. Be sure to mention all the things happening on the farm, such as new buildings, new animals, or new produce you now raise.

Make a photo book with pictures of all the different groups that visited you. This book is a great tool for selling to new groups. If you are able to make a personal presentation, bring the book with you to show off the beauty of your farm, and the excitement of sharing the farm experience with city dwellers. If you need to send pictures through the mail, be sure to select a winning group of pictures that would make anyone want to visit. Write a letter that clearly describes your amenities, from visiting the draft horses in the barn to feeding the geese at the pond.

Sign a contract with every group that sets foot on your property. One part of the contract protects you from legal consequences of anyone being hurt on your property and should be drawn up or reviewed

by a lawyer. The other part specifically mentions
things like:

1. Time and date of the rental, including arrival
   time and departure times and overtime fees.
2. Responsibilities of the renter and the rentee.
   An example: "Sweet Song Ranch will provide
   6 picnic tables and 2 portapotties. The AllCity
   Corporation will provide all food and drink for
   its employees."
3. Staffing needs—who will serve, clean up, and
   so on.
4. Who will haul away the garbage.
5. Parking restrictions or requirements.

Mention that your farmhouse will not be open to
tours; otherwise, you may have a problem with visitors camping out in your kitchen. A written contract makes everything clear, while a verbal contract
leaves the door open for later disgruntlement.

Keep all the congratulatory letters that groups
send to you. If you do not receive a glowing letter
from a group, be sure to write or phone them for
their comments. If they have some gripes, make
sure to hear them all out, both to alleviate their
feelings and to understand how you can avoid any
mistakes the next time. If they are happy with
their experience, ask them for referrals to other
companies.

A rose grower in Petaluma, California, put together an especially smart scheme to supplement
his business. Because he is close to a number of
urban areas and right off a connecting freeway, he
has the perfect location for maximizing his sidelines. Ray Reddell runs the Garden Valley Ranch as
a very diverse operation that brings in profits all year

long. He grows rose plants that he sells bare root or potted up out of a quaint old farm lean-to on the property. He sells the blooms from his permanent beds to restaurants in San Francisco. And he takes advantage of his beautiful site by offering a special area to rent for parties and weddings.

A small outbuilding houses a reheat kitchen, not a code kitchen, and multiple bathrooms. Ray's business parking lot provides ample and convenient space for the cars of partygoers. The party area is rented out by the hour for receptions hosted by the neighboring college, for weddings amid the roses, and for birthday celebrations throughout the nice-weather times of the year. He has gone to the effort of landscaping a tract near the kitchen into a beautifully designed fragrant garden, and a big grassy space on the other side is perfect for dancing or strolling.

Ray has to pay the staffing costs to keep the grounds picture perfect, but because he runs a retail outlet on the property, he has to do this anyway, so party rentals don't cost him extra time and effort to spruce the place up just before the event. He carries liability insurance as a matter of course because the public comes to the nursery every day.

With the right location, you can market to a number of different groups. Investigate hosting school trips, botany class collecting trips, and club outings. A retail outlet, U-pick business, or roadside stand is a perfect way to target your audience for rental of your party site. Displaying a sign that announces the availability of your site for events, having a book with photographs next to the cash register, and talking to people as they visit your property are effective, inexpensive marketing tactics.

FESTIVALS

Festivals are an exciting way to bring city people to the farm. Families or groups of friends will drive sixty to eighty miles to attend a festival. You can celebrate a holiday such as Mother's Day, ring in the summer equinox, hold a pumpkin patch weekend, or host an old-fashioned farm day with corn shucking, apple peeling, hayrides, and cider pressing. You can target family outings, but don't neglect the possibility of senior tours, bus trips for visiting tourists, and schoolchildren.

Wooden Shoe Bulb Company of Mount Angel, Oregon, welcomes visitors to their spring tulip show every year. Sightseers can wander out through the fields and purchase freshly cut tulips to take home or to ship anywhere in the United States. Next to the garden store, Wooden Shoe Bulb has planted beds with each tulip species labeled for the convenience of shoppers ordering bulbs from the catalog. The garden store sells hats, polos, and sweatshirts, as well as a variety of other small items.

The owners use their fall catalog to announce the approximate dates of next spring's show, with the caveat to call and check for peak bloom, which may change depending on the weather. Small advertisements in neighboring papers reach people not on their mailing lists. Their most successful advertising is the free television and newspaper coverage they get as a spot of local color.

Although the tulip show is quite labor intensive for the Iverson family, the retail sales of fresh tulips and bulb orders it generates have become a major sideline to the family business of wholesale blooms and bulbs for the nursery trade.

The Amish community outside of Boise, Farmer Brown's Farm, celebrates with a pumpkin festival every year. They carefully take advance reservations from schools all during the week so they can control the flow of children for their safety and make sure enough pumpkins are available. Students have a chance to visit the rabbits, kept in a big walk-in pen. Then they ride out in a horse-drawn haywagon to choose their pumpkins. Farmer Brown's charges $2 for the ride; the pumpkin is free. They have set the price of the ride to be equivalent to the cost of a supermarket pumpkin, but obviously, the kids will have so much fun that the value of the event is perceived to be greater than the price of a store-bought pumpkin.

The community of Farmer Brown's puts a lot of planning into how the farm looks. They carefully plant sunflowers around the edge of the fields for visual appeal, maintain the old farm buildings, and use horse power for mechanical needs. They offer catered dinners, complete with hayrides and barbecues. The community has plans to create a working historical farm, and runs after-school 4-H programs and summer programs for children.

Full Belly Farm in Guinda, California, has a community sustained agriculture program (CSA), and in connection with that, they hold an open house and party called "Hoes Down." The all-day event offers lots of fun farm activities, so if you are making the two-hour drive from the Bay Area, you know that you have a full schedule of activities to enjoy. There are tours of neighboring farms, old-fashioned farming activities, music, food, and an after-dinner dance. This event brings together those people buying their food through the CSA program and farmers' markets, introduces them to potential new buyers, and attracts media from all over Northern California.

Gizdich Ranch in Watsonville, California, hosts

tours of its apple orchards as a sideline to its U-pick
operation of strawberries, brambles, and apples.
Nita Gizdich has been doing tours with children for
ten years, and her system is well organized. She
begins to book her tours in August and has school
groups lined up from September through November.
She handles one bus tour each hour from 9 A.M. to
2 P.M., with a charge of $1.50 per person. The school
provides one adult volunteer for each five children
on the tour. The children each pick five apples, putting them on the assembly line and watching as the
apples are washed and graded. They sample cider
and learn how it is made and work on identifying
five different varieties of apples grown at the ranch.
Before leaving, everyone picks one apple to take
home. Nita loves leading the tours and is convinced
that she is educating future consumers. Often, the
kids are back several weekends later with their parents, so she is also convinced that she has an effective marketing technique.

COMMUNITY SUSTAINED AGRICULTURE

A revised version of the children's story "The Little
Red Hen" describes one of the most exciting new
developments in farming today. As you'll recall, the
Little Red Hen asked all her friends to help her grow
the wheat, mill the wheat, and then bake the bread,
but they refused. When those fragrant fresh bread
aromas floated over the barnyard, all those unwill-
ing workers turned up to share the treat, but the
Little Red Hen turned them away and ate the bread
by herself. Well, today, farmers are asking for help,

but unlike the hen and her friends, are making the barnyard a scene of shared harvest.

Community sustained agriculture is becoming one of the most alluring ways to provide your farm with income as well as regular, dependable outlets for your farm products. A subscription farm operates on a very simple system with a number of local variations. Basically, you sell shares to your farm's harvest in the coming season. Your shareholders' fee covers seed, input, and living costs until the harvest. Together, you and your shareholders set prices and regulations, usually at local retail costs. The shareholder feels a part of farm life, experiences the satisfaction of raising food, and can often enable you to reduce labor costs. You provide a once-a-week distribution of fruits and vegetables for each family. Some farms are becoming cooperatives, and by joining together are able to offer their shareholders meat, eggs, poultry, honey, fruits, vegetables, and flowers. If one of your crops fizzles, the disaster is borne equally by all your shareholders.

Originating in Europe, CSA is a national movement with over 200 farms participating all over America. There are now CSA farms throughout Europe, Japan, and Canada. To succeed, your farm needs to be located near an urban center with participants eager to farm or purchase farm-fresh products.

Most of the CSA farms are organic. Over and over again, the shareholders stress how important it is to them to know where and how their food is grown. Another great attraction for shareholders is the rare opportunity to work together with their children. They see CSA as an important way to teach children the value of the land and the joy of harvest.

Some of the farms are not yet profitable, but they are at least breaking even. Farmers supplement their income by selling excess crops at farmers' markets and other outlets. Sometimes crops are too small to be distributed equally to all the shareholders, and these too can be sold for extra profit. Continued communication between you and the shareholders is crucial to the success of CSA. Many farms put on festivals, dinners, or workdays to assure the growth of a mutual vision.

This system of farming, like any system, may not be for everyone, or even for you, but it is a significant development. If you hear of a farm in your area that is a CSA, take the time to go over and see the operation in order to measure its effectiveness. Small farmers who were about to lose their farms, or to give up farming because they were not able to find the niche to support them, have become the prime spokespeople for the movement, in gratitude to the renewed opportunity to continue their way of life on the farm.

EDUCATION PROGRAMS WITH CITY SCHOOLS

School groups are visiting farms all over America to learn about agriculture, history, and food production. With some outreach effort, you may be able to start a connection that pays for itself in community relations and fees.

FarmHands-CityHands is one of the best-known organizations that links farmers and school programs. This nonprofit agency arranges for executives, business people, and city children to visit farms surrounding New York City. The original impetus for the program was to bring helpers from the cities to the farmers with crops needing harvesting. Now the goodwill the organization fosters draws adults and kids into an agricultural environment, where they learn how food grows and develop a taste for good, fresh food. Wendy Dubit, the executive director, has gone on to nurture many different levels of relationships, from inner-city kindergartners to corporate executives, chefs, and food brokers. She works to build an understanding of the role of farming to bring food to the table, to encourage an appreciation of the environment, as well as to highlight the regional foods, from cheeses to wines, preserves, and produce.

Many other areas have special school programs, bringing small 4-H groups or whole classes to farms. Farmer Brown's, outside of Boise, welcomes busloads of kids by reservation, and they plan to work closely with the schools as they continue to develop their living-history farm. They find the children often bring their parents back on the weekends, when they have a petting zoo and a farmers' market. The kids have become marketing experts for them.

ON-FARM RESEARCH

With the growth of small farms, part-time farmers, and alternative farming methods, agricultural experts have an unprecedented opportunity to test their theories on successful working farms. The amount of funding for on-farm research is quite small as yet (see Resources at the end of the chapter for some possible sources), but interest in academic circles is growing, and it may be something you will want to pursue. If there is an agricultural college near you, give them a call to see whether anyone is interested in working with you.

On-farm research may require you to take extra time to carefully document your procedures, but you will be paid for your trouble, and you may discover new sources of information invaluable to your farm. Sometimes you can approach different agencies to help you test a project you have in mind. If you are lucky, they will come to you with some research they want done.

Some funds are available for sustainable and organic agriculture, but in certain cases, nonprofit funds can be given only to other nonprofit organizations, so you may have to work with a nonprofit to receive funding. Still, more foundations are getting interested in farming and in the farm-to-city link, so working with a nonprofit group to bring city children out to your farm might be an effective proposal.

You can see that there are a number of ways you can develop your farm to profit from the fact that your lifestyle is exotic to a city person. In a nation where most people live in metropolises, depending on a small number of country people to produce their food, it seems obvious that these two communities need to work together. Because we are rapidly approaching the second generation of children who have never lived on a farm, or never known anyone who lived on a farm, we need to educate them so they will know where food comes from. The story of the child who assumes tomatoes grow in cans may be apocryphal, but farmers who are working with agricultural literacy will tell you many similar stories that are true.

RESOURCES

California Foundation for Agriculture in the Classroom
1601 Exposition Blvd., FB 16
Sacramento, CA 95815
916/561-5699
www.cfaitc.org

Farm Hands-City Hands
Wendy Dubit, Executive Director
34 Downing Street
New York, NY 10014
212/627-HAND

Stankus, Jan. *How to Open and Operate a Bed & Breakfast Home.* Old Saybrook, Conn: Globe Pequot, 1992.

A thorough analysis of everything you need to know, from regulations to pillow mints.

Wooden Shoe Bulb Co.
P.O. Box 127
Mount Angel, OR 97362
800/711-2006
www.woodenshoe.com

Possible Funding Sources for On-site Farm Research:

Organic Farming Research Foundation
Bob Scowcroft, Executive Director
P.O. Box 440
Santa Cruz, CA 95601
831/426-6606

Small Business Innovation Research
USDA Office of Grants
Stop 2243, Aerospace Center
1400 Independence Avenue S.W.
Washington, DC 20250-2243
202/401-4002
www.reeusda.gov/sbir

UC Sustainable Agriculture and Education Program
University of California, Davis
Davis, CA 95616-8176
530/752-7556

Funding for California projects only.

USDA SARE (Sustainable Agriculture Research and
Education) North Central Region
University of Nevada, Lincoln
13-A Activities Building
Lincoln, NE 68583
402/472-7081

USDA SARE Northeast Region
Department of Plant and Soil Science
University of Vermont
Hills Building
Burlington, VT 05405
802/656-2630

USDA SARE Southern Region
Agricultural Experiment Station
University of Georgia
Griffin, GA 30223
707/412-4788

USDA SARE Western Region
Utah State University
4865 Old Main Hill
AgScience, Room 305
Logan, Utah 84322
435/797-2297

CHAPTER 8

Great Ideas for City Gardeners

City gardeners can make money in their backyards. Crops from a plot as small as forty square feet can provide an income to pay off household bills or contribute to a vacation fund. Space limitations can be overcome with a number of creative solutions. Backyard gardeners grow crops in raised beds, produce bushels of fruit by planting hedges of dwarf fruit trees, and plant specialty vegetables and herbs in containers. These methods provide the city dweller with a harvest that merits a stall in a farmers' market, a monthly meal at a favorite restaurant, or sales from a local specialty grocery store. You can plan a year-round production cycle or a seasonal harvest, depending on your space, your crops, and your available time and interest. Don't be afraid of using your front yard for herbs, an open porch for containers of hanging tomatoes, or a shady north side yard for lettuce in the heat of the summer. Experiment to use every inch of space you have.

FINDING THE ROOM

Enterprising growers can rent the backyards of neighbors who are uninterested in gardening (perhaps for a payment of vegetables). Some gleaners note fruit trees blooming in neighbors' backyards, and they check with the owners about harvesting the fruit. Many city dwellers find their backyard fruit trees troublesome to prune and messy with fruit drop. To these people, the barter of tree care for harvest rights becomes a welcome relief from hauling out ladders and raking up rotting fruit. Growers are experimenting with a number of fruit production techniques that use smaller trees planted closely together, in contrast to conventional orchards. Farmers espalier trees grafted onto dwarf rootstock to four-to-six-foot-high trellises, or they run them like grapevines supported by horizontal wires. The backyard farmer can prune dwarf trees along a property line, squeezing at least ten trees along a thirty-foot fence line. The trees bear earlier, are easier to pick and prune, and bear good quantities of fruit in a small space.

More ambitious growers lease land from farmers on the fringe of the city. This helps those just starting out establish a reputation and learn the trade without the capital expenditure of a land purchase. Make arrangements for water use and for a guaranteed number of seasons, because your investment in your soil conditioning will be a cost that you will not want to be forced to repeat if you suddenly lose your lease.

WHAT TO GROW IN
YOUR MARKET GARDEN

The first step in designing your backyard harvest is to look at your market opportunities. As an urban gardener, you can grow for specialty markets right in your neighborhood. You may not be able to

match the volume of the larger farms and wholesalers, but you can offer unusual items unavailable
to stores and restaurants through the regular distribution channels. Remember what you can provide
for your buyers: custom produce picked at the very
peak of ripeness and flavor. Because you are conve-
niently close by, you can deliver more often than
larger businesses.

Design your crop schedules around unusual varieties and include those that harvest very early or
very late; do not duplicate what everyone can buy
all over town. Green Grape tomatoes are a better
choice to grow than Sweet 100's, because wholesalers sell the Sweet 100's, while the Green Grapes are
much harder to find. Can you deliver fresh cherries
long after the market has sold out by researching
rare varieties? Look into the ethnic markets for
possible sales. If you can grow fresh cilantro and
tomatillos, check with Mexican restaurants to see
whether they would be interested in buying from
you directly. The local Asian grocery store or restaurant might order pea tendrils. Asian herbs are
often easy to grow but rarely found at wholesalers,
so you may get an enthusiastic welcome when you
offer a steady supply.

No matter what you are growing, make sure to
line up buyers for your products before they are
ripe. Remember, many businesses order produce
once a month, or they will place a monthly order
with deliveries on a weekly or bimonthly basis. Apples and oranges can be stored longer than the more
perishable herbs and lettuces, but your buyer may
have already ordered when you show up with your
just-picked, fresh produce. Regardless of the quality of your product, if the buyer has made an order,
you have lost a customer.

A friend with a backyard tree had an unexpected

problem with a family of squirrels devouring her apple crop. To foil them, she picked the tree clean, ending up with about a hundred pounds of apples. When she called to sell to her neighborhood grocer who always bought out the crop, he regretfully refused because he had too many apples in stock. She had to go out and find another buyer. This backyard grower learned the hard way to plan ahead and market the apples before they needed to be eaten.

Anne Webster, of Oakland, California, grew for the chef of a nearby restaurant for many years. When she purchased her house, she discovered her long narrow lot was filled with fruit trees, among them a prolific navel orange tree. A superb gardener, she experimented with different crops to come up with a mix of fruits and vegetables she could grow and sell over a long period of harvest. She grew specialty lettuces spring, summer, and fall, blackberries and raspberries, the sweet navel oranges, herbs, and edible flowers. The chef designed specialty dishes around Anne's fruits and vegetables, knowing in advance when her crops were going to arrive in his kitchen. A florist friend checked Anne's yard regularly to purchase many of the vegetables that Anne allowed to go to seed, such as chard with long seed stalks, the blue thistle blooms of artichokes, bronze fennel with lacy foliage and seed heads, and long whips of wisteria, both in leaf and as bare tendrils.

Cut Flowers

If you love flowers, you might try growing special varieties for florists. Florists usually depend on the wholesale flower markets for the flowers and plants they sell to customers. These flowers are usually standard varieties, however, so florists love finding sources of unusual blooms. Successfully growing cut flowers for florists depends on establishing a relationship with a business and growing specifically what they will purchase. Some florists have developed sidelines of dried flower arrangements and wreaths, and they welcome things they can dry themselves or purchase already dried. Some bulbs potted in special containers can be grown to order for florists by backyard gardeners with little ground space except driveways or patios.

To find other markets for your cut flowers, check with restaurants, caterers, and party planners. These people need quantities of flowers, which you can enlarge with unusual plant materials such as nasturtiums, fig leaves, or the burgundy leaves of plum trees. Don't forget that your local realtor might want to buy flowers or rent plants from you to brighten up rooms during open houses. Supply a restaurateur with a number of small table bouquets or potted bulbs for a steady business.

Fresh Herbs

Most produce departments recognize their customers' rising interest in fresh herbs, and although large-scale farmers are planting to fill the need, there is room for the backyard entrepreneur. Herbs are very simple to grow. Health food stores and medicinal herbal stores are particularly eager for organic herbs, so if you decide you want to grow herbs, be sure to consider organic production.

Chives and garlic can be grown for two crops. The chive leaves are sold for seasoning; the blossoms are harvested for edible flowers. Garlic can be thinned in the spring for green garlic, and harvested later in the summer for the garlic bulb. Look to see what the local markets and health food stores are selling, and ask the produce managers which other herbs they would offer if you made them available.

Herbs lend themselves to a variety of value-added products, such as herb butters, herb vinegars and oils, and dried herb blends. Your local health department will provide the regulations to follow to produce these; the income from the product may make it worth the extra effort.

Nursery Starts, Potted Plants, and Little Herb Plants

Raising plants from seeds takes skill and patience, but for those who have the knack, raising and selling starter plants is a great way to make money in a small space. Check first whether you have to apply for a nursery permit or license in order to sell your plants legally, because certain states regulate the resale of plants.

Order your seeds early, choosing varieties that will not be available in the local nurseries and grocery stores. Unusual vegetables, particularly tomatoes appropriate for your climate, herbs, easy flowers, and houseplants are always very popular. In France, sidewalk vendors put together attractive baskets of herbs for city dwellers. You can offer a special fee to replant these baskets once every two months or so to attract return customers.

Some city vendors have particular luck selling hanging planters festooned with a variety of lettuces and edible flowers. Try combinations of nasturtiums and herbs or a type of cherry tomato that will spill over the sides of the basket. Fill containers with an Asian mix of cilantro, basil, and mint, or an Italian combo of basil, oregano, and marjoram. Ask your customers what they would like you to sell, or offer custom container planting.

Chile Ristas, Garlic Braids, and Christmas Swags

Even though you live in a city, there are things you can grow and make into value-added products you can sell. If your climate is right, you can grow and dry chilies all summer long. Stringing the colorful chilies together with bay leaves for accents makes a good salable product. Garlic will grow in backyards planted close together, and harvested bulbs, once dried, are easy to braid or weave into a wreath. Many people prefer a braid smaller than those found in stores, so make yours in different sizes for different tastes.

When Christmas comes, almost everyone sells wreaths, so you face less competition if you offer custom-produced evergreen swags, which are long chains of greens linked together with wire and ornamented with ribbons or pine cones. Swags are very easy to make, but there are not many people producing them. Check with friends or neighbors who have evergreen trees they may want trimmed, or plan to visit a national forest to harvest greens if you need an inexpensive source. Remember to take out the proper permits before harvesting (see Chapter 4).

Get started in October putting together a customer list of people who will contract with you for their holiday swags. Don't forget realty offices, doctors' offices, and gift shops that will be decorating for the season. Check with florists to see whether they would like to subcontract with you. Measure the length your customers will need to hang the swag around doorways, fireplaces, or up banisters, and figure your price by the foot. Ribbons and pine cones can be charged separately.

Jams and Jellies

If you have fruit trees in your backyard, you may develop a talent for jams and jellies simply by trying to use up all the fruit. Some city entrepreneurs have started a small business of selling freshly made jams and jellies to restaurants and specialty stores. Health code laws apply to these products, so you must make your jams and jellies in an approved kitchen (see Chapter 5). In the city, code kitchens in churches and schools are usually close by. Dried apple wreaths, fruit leathers, and dried fruit pieces are other value-added products that will add to the harvest.

Do not neglect to check with your neighbors to see whether they would like to trade product for the harvest of their trees. Lots of people long for fresh jam, but they have no interest in picking their plums and cooking them down. You will do them a service and harvest free fresh fruit for your enterprise.

Beekeeping

City beekeepers tuck hives on garage rooftops, inside sheds with special bee exits and entrances, and even in sheltered front yards. With the abundance of ornamental flowers and trees that bloom in the city, these urban bees often have an easier time collecting pollen and producing honey than their country cousins. An established beehive can easily produce 125 pounds of honey a year, and sweet, fresh honey sells well. Comb honey is very simple to produce and brings a premium price sold as a delicacy or a medicinal. Beekeepers who want more than one or two hives have no problem storing hives at nearby farms, and the farmer usually considers the payment of a honey supply sufficient for rent.

Honey is not the only reason to keep bees. As pollinators, bees are invaluable to farmers. Beekeepers rent out hives to farmers to ensure successful pollination and subsequent large fruit crops. Although you must figure in the cost of moving your hives after the orchard finishes blooming, the rental sum far exceeds your costs. You have the added reward of being paid to have your bees produce all the honey and beeswax you can sell. The beeswax is easily removed and cleaned at the time you harvest your honey, and you can make it into candles or sell it as a separate product.

In the spring, as a natural process of increasing bee populations, hives divide, and these swarms can be another source of income. Swarm removal can be complicated; you may get calls to remove swarms and discover wasps, not honey bees, because people often do not know the difference. Still, collecting honey bee swarms is often very simple, and you will be paid hourly or by the job for bringing home a new hive. Sometimes these hives may be infected with a bee disease, so beekeepers separate and treat new hives.

Once you are familiar with bees and enjoy working with them, you will discover many other people share your interest. Beekeeping clubs can be found in most cities; these are a great way to learn new techniques and also share information about available space for additional hives.

The Backyard Barnyard

Many cities actually allow you to raise animals and birds within the city limits, provided certain regulations are followed. Roosters are generally prohibited because they do start crowing long before rush hour, waking up and irritating their neighbors. You will not have the room to make lots of money from livestock, but there are ways that animals can pay for their keep as well as add to your income.

Animals make your backyard a very economical and ecological system. Chickens and rabbits eat weeds, and they add valuable nitrogen to the compost pile. Chickens will also eat all the table scraps, so you never waste any food. Some restaurants will contract for fresh rabbit, but you must, of course, follow your local health department guidelines if you are up to the slaughtering process. Fresh eggs are really a wonder, and duck eggs can be sold to Asian markets. Little quail eggs are charming, and sell as novelties. Even if you are producing only four to six dozen eggs a week, fresh eggs sell at a premium, and the old term *egg money* is not to be taken lightly.

Raising exotic birds such as finches, canaries, parakeets, and cockatiels is a simple project, and many pet stores are happy to have a home breeder to buy from. Bird breeding is fun and can make a sizable contribution to your income; again, you need to check the regulations in your state.

SELLING TO YOUR NEIGHBORS

Selling fresh fruits and vegetables to your neighbors is a good way to make a profit and gives you the pleasure of meeting your neighbors at the same time. Some backyard gardeners have an arrangement whereby they sell baskets of produce to their neighbors. They keep the produce selection very simple, but with herbs, potatoes, fruits, vegetables, and flowers, the basket merits the price. Some city growers are making contact with farmers to fill out the baskets with other products such as eggs, syrups, or fruit.

One family grows pumpkins for neighborhood children. The kids come in early summer to choose a baby pumpkin; each one is labeled with the child's name. On the first Sunday of every month until harvest, the owners can come to inspect their pumpkins' growth. At harvesttime, the kids pick and weigh their pumpkins, paying slightly above supermarket prices but leaving very happy. These backyard farmers never have any pumpkins left over.

One backyard herb grower in Oakland, California, is investigating funding her beginning herb business by selling produce grown by regional farmers to her neighbors. This modified version of a community sustained agriculture system guarantees a weekly delivery of produce right to the door, a real boon for busy city workers and seniors who have difficulty getting to the grocery store.

CUSTOM GARDENING

Custom vegetable gardening is a job that can pay off for the city farmer. Many folks would like to start a vegetable garden but they aren't sure how to begin, what varieties to grow, or how many plants to set in. Everyone knows a beginning gardener who started off with five squash plants and ended up begging neighbors, friends, and relatives to take some squash. Anyone who contracts with Lisa Monckton of Yolo County, California, is assured of getting a successful harvest from his or her own backyard. Lisa started a part-time gardening business to put in vegetable gardens for city people who felt too inexperienced or too busy to take the time to get one going for themselves. Lisa starts the plants in her own garden, and then after doing extensive soil preparation in the client's yard transfers in the medium-size plants.

Lisa charges by the square foot, including soil preparation and plantings. She purposely started her prices low in order to attract new customers, and she hopes as she gets established to replant her gardens to take advantage of all her time spent on soil preparation. Although she started her marketing with flyers and newspaper coverage, she hopes to start teaching vegetable gardening classes as a way of meeting new clients.

GARDENING CLASSES

If you love gardening and raising vegetables, your enthusiasm will make you a great teacher. Most city people didn't grow up on a farm, and looking out at the weeds shooting up in their backyard in early spring, they feel overwhelmed. For these new gardeners, books on edible landscaping and demonstration gardens are helpful, but taking a class is a surefire way of getting a good start in a lifelong pursuit for pleasure as well as food production. Developing the professional reputation you need to start teaching courses at nurseries and garden shows may take some time. The best route is volunteer work at botanical gardens or community gardens. Cooperative extension services offer "Master Gardener" classes, and that kind of credential helps launch you on the lecture circuit.

Gardening in the city is not quite like planting ten acres, but do not let the size stop you. Starting small in your own backyard is the exact path hundreds of successful entrepreneurs have followed, and you will learn quickly whether you enjoy fooling around in the garden or want to seriously pursue an agricultural career. No matter how limited your earnings, if you are learning how to grow a product, researching your markets, and developing customers, you are practicing all the skills you will need to expand to a larger farm. You may find that you can produce all the crops you want with the convenience of shops, movies, and town life still right in the neighborhood, or you may be laying the groundwork to a major move on to a farm in the country.

RESOURCES

Association of Specialty Cut Flower Growers
155 Elm Street
Oberlin, OH 44074

Sturdivant, Lee. *Growing and Marketing Cut Flowers.* Friday Harbor, Wash.: San Juan Naturals, 1992.

Sturdivant, Lee. *Profits from Your Backyard Herb Garden.* Friday Harbor, Wash.: San Juan Naturals, 1988.

Wallin, Craig. *Backyard Cash Crops: The Source Book for Growing and Marketing Specialty Plants.* Bellingham, Wash.: Homestead Design, 1992.

CHAPTER 9

Bureaucratic Hurdles

No matter how big or small your growing area is, because you are producing food, there will be government officials looking over your shoulder. If your annual sales are less than $5,000, you will probably be exempt from certification costs for organic. *Anyone* who sells at a farmers' market, however, will still need to spend some nights over paperwork. The small-time jam maker preserving the backyard plum tree's goodness is up against the local health department for production in a code kitchen. If you have country land and are growing a variety of goods, you have even more bosses.

A farmer's land was once a private domain. All the activities, crops, animals, and buildings were under the sway of the property owner. Now farms are subject to as many regulations as corporations are. Rural life is not an escape from red tape. At each juncture of your business planning, you had better clear your plans with the appropriate agencies, although sometimes you will have a hard time knowing which ones those are.

For example, suppose you get together with some friends for dinner, and by dessert you've hatched a grand scheme to start a for-fee pond fishing sideline to your farm. Your location is great, you love to eat fish, and you are sure you have a winning idea. In New York State, you would need the following:

Application for fishing preserve license

Farm fish pond license (must be upgraded prior to allowing fee fishing)

Fish tags permit

Permits to raise fish for breeding, stocking, or resale

Private bass hatchery permit, and/or permit to raise and sell trout

Furthermore, when you dam up a stream you may run into both state and federal agencies that regulate water rights as well as wildlife and conservation issues. If you want to put up a little building to sell coffee and soft drinks, then you will have to go to the zoning and planning boards. If your friends want to open a charming little lakeside café, the health department will get involved. You will be calling your insurance agent to make sure you have a very good liability policy, because if little Harry falls into the pond and swallows a fish and is rushed off to the hospital, you may be liable. If you want to hire someone to help you clean the pond, you will be facing labor taxes, Social Security, and a host of other paperwork.

Check up on restrictions, because infringements can mean sizable fines. In California, EB 198 sets out very stringent rules about safety education for all farm workers. With even one worker, you will be obliged to hold safety meetings in the language of that employee, and your worker must sign a form stating that the session was held. Fines are quite large if an inspection reveals you neglected your meetings.

Staying on top of all the different agencies and their rules is tough. Every regulation is open to interpretation, and that interpretation changes from

year to year, situation to situation. As you thread
your way through sticky situations, remember that
a positive attitude helps resolve a lot of problems.
Nothing makes a difficult situation impossible so
quickly as an angry bureaucrat.

Read the regulations yourself if you run up
against a "no." Find out what else has been happening in your county that is an exception to the rule.
Get to know the planning commissioners, the
county board of supervisors, the local tourist board,
and anyone else involved, and enlist them to help
you find solutions to a problem. Never forget that
the receptionists at the front desk are the gatekeep-
ers, and working with them opens doors to decision
makers. Often, those front desk people know more
about procedures than anyone else, and if you are
looking for real answers, check there first.

FEDERAL AND STATE AGENCIES

USDA (Department of Agriculture)

The first agency to consult is the office of the U.S.
Department of Agriculture in your state. The USDA
is a federal agency that regulates farming throughout the nation. It is a source for federal standards
governing your farm and business, and it has access
to an amazing amount of information and can guide
you to written materials and experts from all over
the country.

Pesticide Regulations

Because pesticides kill things, they are dangerous
materials. Both the state and federal government
have regulations restricting and guiding their use.

Pesticides widely available to the public have instructions on the label that tell you how to use them and what plants you use them on. To use them in ways other than those stated on the label is a violation of the law. Should something occur because of your misuse of chemicals, you will be legally responsible. Be sure to read the labels carefully.

For restricted chemicals, which means those sold only to certified users such as licensed farmers and industries, there are exacting federal and state regulations. These regulations guide how the chemical can be applied to plants and what protective measures the person applying the chemical must take. In some states, among them California, you must secure an application license to handle certain pesticides. Regulations vary by state, so check with your county agent and the EPA. Some states require 100 percent reportage with detailed information on application quantities and crops sprayed. Read the rules about the interval you must wait after spraying before selling your produce. Because of the health risks, you should take the time to learn about pesticide application and the precautions to follow.

Soil Conservation Service, USDA

Soil conservation is a critical problem in American agriculture. This federal organization works with individual farmers on such matters as soil erosion control and flood control. On a county-by-county basis, they offer free soil maps showing the location of soil types. This information is invaluable when purchasing land. On staff throughout the nation are engineers, soil scientists, biologists, agronomists, foresters, and range conservationists, all available to advise you, the private landowner. Irrigation engineers work with you to improve your irrigation techniques and efficiency, saving water and expense, and maintaining water quality.

Nutrition Labeling and Education Act of 1990

The Act, which is scheduled to go into effect in May 1994, sets out restrictions and standards for the text of food labels. For processors of value-added products, the Act necessitates changes in labels. Small producers with food sales of less than $50,000 a year or total sales of less than $500,000 a year are exempted from parts of the Act, however. The Act calls for a nutrition panel on the label, listing total calories, calories from fat, total fat, saturated fat, and so on. As a producer with sales under $50,000 you may be exempt from the nutrition panel, but you are not exempt from correct usage of descriptive words such as "fresh," "free," "low," or "more." Check with the Government Printing Office, Superintendent of Documents, at 710 North Capitol Street NW, Washington, DC 20402, for a copy of the act (GPO number 069-001-00045-9).

Labor Regulations

The U.S. Department of Labor is in charge of all the rules governing working environments. Workers you hire must have proof of citizenship or a green card allowing them to be employed in this country. You pay disability insurance, Social Security, and perhaps a host of other taxes depending on the size of your operation. Children under sixteen not related to the farm operator are considered to be underage, and they are prohibited from working in hazardous operations. You can figure that state and federal laws will cover such topics as minimum wage and taxes, labor housing, and pesticide use.

Commodity Boards for Industry Standards

Commodity boards, sometimes called marketing boards, set industry standards for fruit and vegetable crops, including grades, size, and containers. These boards resulted from farmers banding together to devise ways to supervise and maintain the quality of the harvest. There are both state and federal marketing programs. When you research crops, check to find out what crops are covered by marketing orders, which set out grading sizes, container standards, and selling restrictions. The process for state and federal orders are about the same. If enough farmers want to create an order, they can apply to the Secretary of Agriculture. The secretary will hold hearings to devise an order, where representatives of both the industry and the public testify.

When the law goes into effect, it creates a marketing order and the administrative committee or marketing board to carry out the guidelines in the order. Basically the order does not cover farmers when they are growers. The law regulates produce at the handling point when it is sized, graded, and packed. When you sell a commodity covered by a marketing order, you are assessed by the unit, either a piece or a box, and that money goes to marketing, advertising, and running the marketing board.

Check with your local state or federal Department of Agriculture to find out whether you are excluded from the order, either because of the quantities you sell, or the type of produce you grow.

For federal marketing orders, call

Northwest Marketing Field Office
Portland, Oregon
503/326-2724

California Marketing Field Office
Fresno, California
559/487-5901

Southwest Marketing Field Office
McAllen, Texas
956/682-2833

Southeast Marketing Field Office
Winter Haven, Florida
863/299-4770

Headquarters in Marketing Order
Administration Branch
Washington, DC
202/720-2491

The federal or state Inspection Service in any state should also be able to provide information.

Lady Bird Johnson Highway Beautification Act of 1965

This federal law prohibits any signs within a distance of 660 feet of any federal highway. If you want to advertise your farm stand or U-pick, you must check with your local zoning department to see what requirements you will have to follow. In some states, sign size is regulated except on private property.

Organic Certification

Organic food production is defined as growing food without the use of synthetic fertilizers, herbicides, or pesticides. The claim "organic" can apply to fruit, vegetables, cotton, grains, animal products, dairy products, and fish. The Organic Foods Production Act of 1990 states that a harvest may not be certified organic unless the land the product grows on has had no synthetic inputs for three years. A host of other guidelines and restrictions are continually being defined. Growers wishing to sell produce as organic have to be certified by an independent agency, which will require a map of the location of crops grown, a tally of gross sales, soil samples, lists of crops, lists of everything added to the soil or crop—in short, everything that might affect the organic certification.

Contact your state department of agriculture for the state rules that will continue to be law until the federal act goes into effect.

Water Regulations

State and federal water projects and local irrigation districts govern water purchases by farmers. Unless you use your own well water or surface water, you will need to follow these agencies' regulations.

COUNTY AGENCIES

County Agricultural Commissioner

Most states have county agricultural agents or commissioners, who may be under the federal or state Department of Agriculture. If you need certification for selling in farmers' markets or for beginning the procedure to be certified organic, the county department of agriculture is the place to go. In some cases you are charged a fee for certification, and the certification must be updated yearly. Check with the department in your county for the appropriate regulations.

County Extension Agents

Some states have a county extension service, linked to the land grant colleges and designated as the public advisers for the academic community.

Every state has its own department of agriculture as well. The state government regulates situations not covered by the federal department. Make sure you learn your state regulations, and also find out what kind of help your state agriculture department offers. Often they will have lots of pamphlets that can give you very helpful information applicable to your specific area and needs.

Your local extension agent can suggest crops that grow successfully in the county, and can refer you to farmers' markets and advisers in other agricultural agencies. Because county agents work with teachers on the college faculties, they are often in touch with experts who can advise you on special projects or problems.

Zoning Departments

High on the list of agencies taking an active interest in your land are the county zoning departments. Zoning regulations vary from state to state and from county to county. With zoning regulations come taxes, and it is critical to check what zoning regulations cover your farm. If you are opening a U-pick operation, will you have to be zoned commercial? Usually, commercial zoning comes with a whole set of requirements and a higher tax rate. Some states have a zoning definition called "exclusive farm use," which has a lower tax rate. Many farm operations prefer not to incur a zoning change, because there are a number of restrictions as well as taxes that often result. A zoning change has the long-term effect of transforming an agricultural district into one poised for urban development, spelling the end to your rural activities.

Planning Departments

Planning departments carry out the instructions of the zoning boards; you file your plans for any new construction with your local planning department. They go over your blueprints with a fine-tooth comb to make sure they're up to code. Whether you are installing bathrooms for your U-pick or building a simple unstaffed roadside stand, you'd better check with your planning department to stay within your legal rights. If your construction is not up to code, you will have to strip away as much of the building as the inspectors require.

County Health Department

The health department is the county agency in charge of maintaining sanitary conditions. It has some latitude in protecting citizens, and you need to understand the regulations governing farm health and public health. The health department has the legal right to shut down your kitchen, farm, market stall, or farm stand if it feels you have the potential to cause a public health hazard. The health department is in charge of licensing kitchens, and issues strict guidelines for code kitchens in which you process food for resale. Reheat kitchens have different guidelines, so if you are not preparing food on the premises, you may qualify for a reheat kitchen with less stringent ordinances.

In some areas, the health department has cracked down on growers at farmers' markets cutting and slicing their produce to give samples to customers.

In California, market associations are working with health departments to come up with procedures that will alleviate their concerns. One solution is the building of a code kitchen that could be used for a number of purposes at the market, including the cutting of samples. If you are selling at a market, check on how your market handles sampling.

Department of Weights and Measures

To weigh out produce, either at your on-farm U-pick or at the farmers' market, you must have the measuring device certified for accuracy. The county commissioner certifies your scale and issues a certificate. Some farmers' markets file a copy of the certificate; others want you to post your certificate.

FARMERS' MARKET REGULATIONS

To sell at a farmers' market, you must apply to the market manager for a copy of the market regulations. Most markets require certification by the county to make sure you grow the crops you want to sell in the markets. In some markets, you need to apply for a certificate to register each type of product you wish to sell. Farmers' markets have very high standards, so read their rules for all produce and products sold there.

PRODUCT LIABILITY INSURANCE

If you sell value-added products, you may have to take out product liability insurance to protect you from any consumer claims of injury or illness. Check with your local public health department and your insurance agent to make sure you are fully covered.

UNIVERSAL PRODUCT CODE

The Universal Product Code is the bar code of black and white lines with numbers that holds encapsulated information to be scanned by a machine. The UPC has become customary for products sold in larger department stores and grocery stores. If you sell value-added products on a limited basis or in a direct market situation, you will not find a UPC that useful. If you expand your production and place your wares in the grocery chains, then you will need to add a code to your label.

The Uniform Code Council manages the distribution of the codes. To get a code, you must apply for membership; your membership fee is assessed on a sliding scale based on your sales volume. The address: Uniform Code Council Inc., 8163 Old Yankee Road, Suite J, Dayton, OH 45458.

This, sadly, is not a complete list of all the bureaucratic hurdles you face. Even at this moment, new regulations are being enacted to protect the health and safety of all Americans. Often, in order to close all the loopholes, some regulations become inordinately unfair and untenable under regional, not national, conditions. Sometimes local enforcers realize the absurdity of the situation, and they will tactfully ignore or adapt the regulation to your needs and conditions.

Remember, everyone is usually very frustrated by red tape, so keep calm, keep smiling, and keep working to find a solution.

CHAPTER 10

Paying the Mortgage: Success Stories from Around America

When all is said and done, farmers farm success-fully throughout America. Tax forms, crop certification, zoning permits, and visits from the health department notwithstanding, farmers keep growing and keep selling. Farming can be solitary, and even if you meet the public, you need time to discuss your problems and solutions with other farmers. Sharing ideas can be a good way to come up with new techniques for growing or marketing your products, and that flexibility to continually assess your farm.

These farmers believe anyone can succeed; they attend farm conferences and work with a variety of groups to share advice and expertise. Every farmer will say farming is a tough job, and each has experienced his or her share of setbacks. But persevere, and you will measure your own successes with pleasure.

Jeanne Jackson, Iron Kettle Farm, Candor, New York

Jeanne and her husband Skip have farmed ever since they left city life just after graduating from college and marrying. They decided that country life was what they wanted, so they moved back to New York State and bought a farm.

Twenty-five years later, Iron Kettle Farm is a family business, with a farm market that brings people out from the surrounding towns all spring, summer, and fall. Their location on the main route to the Finger Lakes district of upper New York gives them a market of summer travelers who need supplies for vacation cabins. The farm now has 150 acres of vegetables, enough to supply the farm store and wholesalers who pick up the product right at the farm.

Jeanne emphasizes that in the beginning they had days when they hardly made $5 at a small roadside table they loaded with produce. Still, with time, they built up a clientele who trusted them, and who came regularly to buy and pick their fruit and vegetables.

Their farm stand is the money-maker, but they also offer U-pick for strawberries, tomatoes, and pumpkins. They have tried different crops through the years, but Jeanne says her customers are only interested in picking these three. She buys apples in the fall for the stand because they cannot grow them in their very cold valley, and she stocks jams, jellies, and cider because her customers asked for them. She is careful not to make the store a grocery store, selling only what is appropriate to a farm stand.

To bring people out from the surrounding towns in the fall, Jeanne created a huge pumpkin display in front of the stand. Every year it gets bigger and bigger, with pumpkin characters of all sorts and shapes. Now the display runs for six weeks, with farm animals, a crafts show, and of course pumpkins everywhere. Jeanne laughs when she describes

how people call to check the dates so they can schedule relatives' visits while the pumpkin display is on.
The display is so well known, people come from all
over the state to see it.

During the pumpkin display, Jeanne buys radio
and newspaper advertising, but she finds word of
mouth is her very best press agent. She feels that
people come back because they know and trust her,
and they are sure of the quality of Iron Kettle Farm.
Longevity is in their favor. She also works very
hard to make the farm and the store particularly
attractive, and in the spring, she arranges flower
displays in huge black kettles at the roadside to
attract passersby and let them know the farm is
open and ready for business.

Like many farmers, Jeanne believes teaching
children about farming is important. Farm animals
are always around for the children to pet. In the
spring, Jeanne has baby ducks and chickens that
she hatches from an incubator. She feels these
animals help her business; school bus tours and
families with small children come for the entertainment they provide.

Jeanne and Skip have recently made Iron Kettle
Farm a family corporation, in partnership with
their two sons and their wives. For the first time,
Jeanne thinks they will need to write a business
plan and set down their goals. Now that three families depend on the farm for income, changes will
need to be made. One of the possibilities being considered is tours, but Jeanne is reluctant to charge
for unguided, informal ones. They may start formal
tours for a fee.

Jeanne recognizes the farm makes money because
its location near a number of small towns gives her
a steady customer base supplementing the summer
tourist trade. She feels her customers' loyalty to her

and appreciation of her efforts to work for them have created a two-way relationship that is the basis of the farm's success. She runs the store to satisfy her customers, and she listens to them and tries different things to make the farm a stop for many families. Staying flexible to revamp her business to suit her customers has worked, and she suggests you look for ways to always keep your customers happy and coming back for more.

Tom McCrumm, South Face Farm, Ashfield, Massachusetts

Come March, steam will be puffing from the sugarhouse on South Face Farm, and Tom McCrumm will be checking his evaporators and vacuum pumps inside. Tom grew up wanting to run a maple syrup operation, and for the last seven years he has been producing about 2,000 gallons of syrup every year in Ashfield, Massachusetts.

With a friend in the early seventies, Tom learned how to tap trees and process the sap. He moved to Virginia and tried sugaring there; returning to Massachusetts, he bought a run-down sugaring farm that had produced maple sugar products for 150 years and started his own business.

Tom says he is one of those who see something broken, figure out what is wrong, and fix it. He set about refitting the worn-out and outmoded sugaring machines and facilities. Keeping the syrup operation going was no small effort, because every January, Tom taps more than 2,500 trees and attaches buckets or tubing to collect the sap. He has about 40,000 feet of plastic tubing that squirrels will chew, and at $65 per thousand feet, that makes expensive food. Every tree, in a good year, will produce ten gallons of sap, which when boiled down yields just one quart of the grade A maple syrup Tom produces and sells for $40 a gallon. In a bad year, the yield goes down, and two out of the last seven years have been bad.

South Face Farm is a destination on sugaring weekends. Families drive out to have breakfast at the little restaurant next to the sugarhouse and watch Tom stirring the big vat of syrup. The restaurant, housed in a forty-year-old farm building, seats 50. Last year, the farm had about 2,000 visitors on the six weekends of the season, and Tom hopes to increase that number in coming years. Snowstorms can strike as late as March and April, and bad weather keeps his visitors away.

When asked, Tom laughs about a business plan, and says he knows he should sit down and make one up. The farm evolved gradually, and because he works as the executive director of the Massachusetts Maple Producers Association, he has picked up tips and marketing ideas from other producers. He goes to conferences and producers' meetings to gather more ideas all the time.

When Tom bought South Face Farm, he figured the business would have a base of customers to get him started. Unfortunately, the bad management of the previous owner had taken its toll. To bring in customers, Tom designed a brochure that he left at the motels and hotels nearby. He put a bucket out front with a pad of paper and a pencil, offering a drawing for a free gallon of syrup, and that became the basis for his mailing list. He sat down at his typewriter and wrote letters to friends of his parents and his own friends, and sent out a simple ordering form. When another sugaring operation shut down, Tom bought its list, and the owner wrote a letter explaining he was going out of business and encouraging his old customers to switch to Tom's product.

Historically, maple sugaring has been an off-season project for farmers during the winter, but Tom sees the business as a year-round operation. Once, when he was asked what he did after sugaring shut down, he gently reminded his questioner that he still had 1,500 gallons of syrup to sell. Marketing is not just a seasonal job for Tom.

Tom is a good marketer. As the head of the Massachusetts Maple Producers Association, he works to get free newspaper publicity for the 100 sugar producers in Massachusetts. Articles announce the beginning of the season, and Tom sends out free trail maps on request. He has joined the Western Massachusetts Food Industry Association, a group of 50 food producers, most of which are small cottage industries.

Several factors make the selling of Massachusetts syrup a tough business. Canadian syrup is cheaper, Vermont syrup is better known. Tom figures his niche is to market his syrup as a "Made in Massachusetts" quality farm product. He arranges with other Massachusetts farmers to sell his product at farm stands and roadside markets. He establishes a rapport, and likes working with other farmers because, as farmers, they appreciate one another's efforts. If someone comes along with a product a couple of cents cheaper, a farmer is not impressed, and will stay with the supplier he knows.

Mail order is important to the business. Tom keeps the list pared down to save expenses. At the sugarhouse, he has a sign-up for his mailing list, but he cautions people against signing up if they are not going to order. He says they like his honesty, and some laugh and sign, and others grin and walk

away. He takes names off the list if they do not
reorder after three years. He is thinking of adding
a May mailing.

When he writes a mailer, he takes the time to tell
people what he has been doing, and what has been
happening on his farm. He feels that because he
sells an expensive item, his customers need to understand his life and costs in order to realize that
they're getting a quality product at a reasonable
price.

From May to October, Tom looks for new products. He puts together gift baskets for the corporate
and business market, adding a pancake mix, and
works with a group to make a Massachusetts-
products basket with mustard, shortbread, and
other food items. To bring this market into better
focus, Tom attends specialty gift shows.

Tom feels a farmer must get into the direct marketing business to be successful. He advises farmers
to sell direct to make the money they deserve for
their hard work. On the other hand, he wants to
educate consumers that they must support Massachusetts agriculture in order to keep open space and
to keep farms in business. If the consumer meets the
farmer, then there will be a communication that benefits both of them.

Chris Holmes, New Penny Farm, Presque Isle, Maine

Potatoes saved Chris Holmes's farm. New Penny
Farm, in Presque Isle, Maine, is in the middle of
80,000 acres of potato-growing land. Up to 1985,
Chris grew "normal" potatoes, but found himself
caught in the bind of raising more and more potatoes for less and less money. When he explored

ways to increase his earnings, he discovered specialty potatoes.

Now the seventy-acre New Penny Farm grows nineteen kinds of heirloom and specialty potatoes on ten acres. Chris farms only that amount because of his organic farm system. He builds up the soil through cover crops and sod building. He came to the conclusion that he wanted to farm organically because, in his words, "relying on chemicals is going up a dead-end road. It may go for a little while, but soon it stops." Farming organically is important to him. He admits that most of his customers don't ask whether he farms organically, but he feels chemical dependence is bad farming.

Chris attributes his success to close attention to his soil. One year of growing potatoes is followed by a year of oats and two years of a grass-clover mixture which he uses as a sod crop for organic enrichment of the soil. He could, of course, farm more land, but building up the soil gives him a resilient potato that fights off diseases such as early blight, and assures high-quality flavor and texture.

Chris's price structure reflects his niche as a specialty producer. Determined to avoid the high volume, low price syndrome, Chris believes that lower yields of better products give him the control to set his own prices. His customers recognize the quality and they willingly pay more. Instead of making 15 to 20 cents a pound, he gets $1.50 to $4 a pound for his special yellow, purple, and pink potatoes.

He carries off marketing with great panache. A friend who had worked in advertising in Boston and New York suggested that Chris try running an advertisement in the New Yorker magazine. The ad appears from October to May, and customers call an 800 number to order. Chris supplements his ad with a mail order catalog, and his mailing list now runs to 7,000 names. A new computer sits on his desk to track mailing addresses, UPS deliveries, credit cards, and orders.

Most of his orders come around Christmas for presents, and he packages his products with this market in mind. To make potatoes a gift item, he puts five pounds in baskets. Order ten pounds and you get a potato barrel. He started a "Potato of the Month" club based on Harry and David's business, originally started in the Depression. Chris maintains that no matter how tough times get, there are people who want quality and who have the money to pay for it.

Chris pays attention to the education of his customers. Purple potatoes have not hit the saucepans of most consumers, so he explains how to cook them and what they will taste like. Starch levels vary with each variety; low-starch varieties are better boiled, whereas high-starch varieties are superb mashed and baked. Growing the potatoes is one thing; making sure the customers enjoy them is the next step. Chris wants his customers to send in repeat orders.

Chris uses other marketing outlets and sells other products to augment his eight-month catalog potato business. He sells a portion of his potato crop to a wholesaler in Boston. His catalog offers items from other producers that have an old-fashioned flavor complementing his potatoes, such as a buckwheat pillow from Quebec and an Acadian pancake mix. Later in the season, he sell fiddleheads he gathers from the riverbanks. Still, it is his nineteen potato varieties that really make a difference, and for Chris Holmes, it is the difference that pays.

Sally Small, Pettigrew Fruit, Walnut Grove, California

Sally Small and her brother Rob work as a team to run Pettigrew Fruit, an orchard on Steamboat Slough in the Sacramento Delta. Their grandfather planted the orchard back in 1911, and the family has been farming on the land ever since. As marketing director, Sally sells the apples and pears while Rob works the farm, with its yearlong schedule of pruning, grafting, planting, training the trees on trellises, and, from mid-June to October, picking the fruit. He uses natural methods, including an integrated pest management system. Codling moths tunnel inside apples, making them inedible, so Rob has hired a university expert to advise Pettigrew Fruit on the problem. The expert's salary is paid from savings accrued from using organic controls instead of purchasing pesticides. Although Pettigrew Fruit is not certified organic, Sally feels the integrated pest management system produces safe food.

Sally and Rob got into the specialty fruit business on a wager with their father in 1981. She bet she could sell the pears from a particular patch in the orchard planted by her grandfather. The trees were slated for firewood, except the pears were the family's favorite. That first year, Sally and Rob packed 250 boxes of French Butter pears. Sally opened the back of her station wagon every day, loaded up, and went out to knock on doors. They had no facilities for cold storage, so she raced to sell every box before the pears became overripe.

Now the family grows French and Italian Butter pears, Granny and Gala apples, and Comice pears and sells 40,000 cases a year through wholesalers to white-tablecloth restaurants like Chez Panisse, chain stores, and specialty food stores throughout the Bay Area. Their culls go to juice processors.

All along, Sally had the help of people in the produce business. She credits their patience, interest, and support for the success of Pettigrew Fruit. She consulted with Bill Fujimoto, the owner of Monterey Market, one of the largest markets of fresh produce in the Bay Area. He taught her how to box the fruit, suggested the tissue wrapping, and helped her with the pricing. She still asks him yearly for pricing advice.

Even the large chain stores have been encouraging, willing to talk to her, and allowing her into the stores to do sampling with customers. Her recommendation is to seek the help of the wholesalers and retailers, and get them on your side. They want quality produce to sell, and in her experience, they are receptive if you are willing to take the time to work with them.

Sally works closely with them, making sure her fruit is properly handled, and that it arrives at its final destination in good condition. She believes more farmers should take the time to find out what happens to their fruit after being handled by lumpers three or four times. She even went to the produce managers in one store to teach them when to sell a Granny Smith. She found that they were selling them before they were ripe, and she had to show them the difference in taste and texture and help them develop maturity standards.

Early on, Sally and Rob decided to go for brand recognition with their fruit. That meant they needed to develop public awareness of the Pettigrew Fruit label. One of the choices they made was to ship in old-fashioned wooden crates, even at a cost of a dollar more per crate than conventional waxed cardboard boxes. The fruit is hand packed, with every pear enfolded in tissue for maximum protection. When you're shipping 10,000 boxes of pears, that's a lot of tissue.

Sally goes to the stores to offer samples of her fruit. To her, passing out samples is not marketing, it is a course in what her customers think and what they buy. She listens to them closely, and takes the time to describe the fruit, its history, its ripening and preparation. Sally swears that every farmer in America should spend one day standing in a market selling what they grow and listening to their buyers. She wants farmers to ask the public whether they want wax on their apples, and to explain how the wax affects the fruit and why the farmers wax them. Sally is convinced that the public has questions for the farmers, and that if the public understood farm practices, there would be more pressure for sustainable agriculture, biological controls, and quality standards.

Sally and Rob are taking a second look at the future of Pettigrew Fruit. They have worked hard to put together a business that provides their permanent employees housing on the ranch, decent wages and health benefits, plus a profit-sharing plan. Working as a cooperative selling their neighbors' fruit has been good for the company in past years, but recently, for the first time, they only broke even, so they may scale back to selling their own fruit only. They plan to continue experimenting with European varieties, testing them in the Delta soil and climate.

Sally says farmers today must realize that although past generations were content to take their satisfaction in the quality of their product, that does not work in the modern marketplace. Today, farmers must be merchandisers as well. If you want to stay in business, you have to sell.

Bill Kilpatrick, The Apple Barn, Sevierville, Tennessee

Can you imagine having so much business that you stop handing out brochures? Bill apologetically admits that his staff goes nuts when the Barn is full and three more tour buses pull up to the front door.

Bill Kilpatrick had no intention of becoming a farmer with a roadside business that brings in over a million visitors a year. He grew up expecting to work in a pharmacy like his father. Accordingly, he went to pharmacy school and opened a drugstore. Then, with some of his friends, he bought an old run-down farm to subdivide. Based on that success, he and a friend found another farm, but this one had a nice farmhouse, was fenced, and came with a big old tobacco barn. Bill remodeled the farmhouse and moved in, raised cattle to keep the grass down, and grew tobacco to keep their farm tenant occupied. Bill thought he might plant some apple trees as a hobby. Hobbies have a way of changing lives.

When Bill had some trouble with the tobacco, he called upon his extension agent to diagnose the problem. During his inspection of the tobacco, the agent saw Bill's orchard and mentioned that an extension agent specializing in fruit trees had been hired, and he invited Bill to a fruit production meeting. The county had at one time been the site of numerous orchards, but tobacco had taken over because of greater profitability. In the 1970s, the price of tobacco dropped, so the extension was encouraging farmers to once again try orchards.

Bill did some investigating and planted about 1,100 trees. A couple of years later, he realized that he was facing an orchard of fruit to sell, and he had better figure out just how. He took a tour of farm markets in Ohio and Michigan and came back with a number of ideas.

He decided to move the cattle out of the barn and set up a cider press. In 1981, he opened up for business with a different variety of apples displayed in every stall, and the press pumping out fresh cider. That first year, he was open only during apple season, about eight weeks, but he had success.

The next year, he began to listen to his customers and added various items they requested when they came to buy apples and cider. Visitors found cookies, a cider bar, aprons, local crafts alongside the apples. Bill placed a guest book at the cash register, and people made more suggestions. They asked for country hams, molasses, and more cider. After closing that year, Bill bought a bigger cider press and enlarged the cider room.

At this time he was still working in his drugstore, but with the success of the Apple Barn, he sold the store and went to work at the hospital pharmacy, until his business got so big he quit to work at it full time.

Bill heard his customers asking where they could go to get a full meal, so in 1986 he and his wife moved out of the farmhouse, remodeled it, and opened a restaurant in 1987. At this point, the Apple Barn was open from summer until Christmas. That winter, Bill decided to remodel and expand the barn. While they were remodeling the barn, people, seeing the activity, continually drove in, only to be disappointed to learn they were closed.

With that hint, Bill made the decision to keep the Apple Barn open all year long. The first winter was slow, but business has increased every year since. The restaurant attracts customers hungry for meals, and after eating they stroll over to the barn. At the

same time, people coming to buy things out of the
barn get hungry, and head to the restaurant.

Bill has opened a candy shop with peanut brittle,
fudge, caramel apples, and apple taffy made in the
shop. He has also added an ice cream shop, and a
pie bakery producing delicious, ready-to-eat products right on the spot. Bill describes a truck driver
who comes to make a delivery, walks into the barn,
and smells the aroma of freshly baked pies. The
trucker leaves with the pie, heading down the interstate. Most of his customers' first words are "Ah,
the aroma."

The mail order business developed because people wrote letters reordering products they had purchased and used. Bill realized he had the chance to
put together another sideline, and now he has three
or four people working all fall and winter shipping
out products all over America.

Bill credits most of his success to his location.
The Apple Barn is alongside the main road to the
Great Smoky Mountains National Park, which
draws 9 million visitors a year; Bill figures 75 percent of them have to go past his business. He has
billboards on the main approaches, and in the fall
he adds some signs just off the interstate.

Bill never solicited tour companies, but suddenly
he found buses passing by on craft or fall color
tours starting to turn in. Tourists piled off the buses
for breakfast, and whenever the barn opened, they
were waiting impatiently outside. Bus tours are a
problem for Bill, because his staff is quickly over-
loaded when three buses come in and the barn is
already filled with visitors. He worries that his employees cannot provide the kind of service he would
like under those circumstances. Because of his level
of business, he has dropped advertising.

Success has created other problems. The Apple

Barn is out in the country, but the closest city annexed his property and zoned it as commercial. Consequently, Bill has been forced to charge a special city tax of 8.5 percent, and to pay a higher property tax.

Bill works very hard to make his operation efficient. Like all thrifty farmers, he uses all his culls and slightly damaged fruit for his cider-pressing operation. In fact, he uses all the apples he grows and buys from neighboring orchards in order to keep his press going to keep up with demand. Taking efficiency one step further, he uses his apple tree prunings to smoke the meat products he sells both in his restaurant and in the barn. After eating the apple-smoked bacon and ham with their eggs and pancakes, everyone wants some apple chips. Bill uses up all his own prunings for his own smoking operation, but he does retail a packaged variety to keep his customers happy.

Keeping his customers satisfied is what Bill says has stretched him in his business. He feels his customers have made his business plan for him, and they are the best business advisers. His customers got him started on the restaurant, they helped him devise his hours and his product list, and they asked him to label everything so they could take souvenirs home from their trips. So aprons have the Apple Barn logo on them, and bottles of sparkling apple juice manufactured by someone else have a label saying they were purchased at the Apple Barn.

Bill remembers when he was starting, the local farmers told him he would never be able to grow apples in the county. Then they told him he could never sell the apples. Now, they are coming by for lunch.

Jim Binsberger, Homestead Orchards, Perkasie, Pennsylvania

Jim works from the premise that for every hour spent on the tractor, a farmer will spend three or four hours on paperwork, dealing with marketing.

Homestead Orchards is about thirty miles from Philadelphia on a little side road in beautiful Bucks County. After an executive career, Jim bought a farm in the country. He began to sell his apples wholesale to a small supermarket. Jim dropped in one night to settle his order with the owner, and noticed that his apples were priced at twice his price to the owner. The next day, while setting up the apples in the display, the owner came to Jim and told him that he would have to buy the apples for 50 cents less than the price he quoted the night before. Jim was annoyed, and refused the offer. The owner tried again, offering to split the price, coming up 25 cents if Jim dropped his price 25 cents. Again, Jim refused. In fact, Jim angrily told the owner that they had made a deal the night before. In disgust, he walked down the aisle to where a shopper was lifting his apples into her cart. He retrieved his apples, telling her the store had refused to buy them. At that moment, Jim vowed never to sell wholesale again.

Jim has developed a very strong marketing plan to sell directly to the consumer and cut out the wholesalers. Besides apples, he sells peaches, pumpkins, and a few specialty items like gourds. Actually, Jim feels he is selling entertainment and agricultural education as well. His billboards on the main road attract customers to the orchards. When they arrive, they find activities for kids, such as hayrides and making scarecrows, so they stay longer. To ensure a crowd, Jim conducts a direct mail campaign, sending 15,000 flyers to a nearby town, choosing a different town every year.

Though Homestead Orchards is close to Philadelphia, it is off the main road, so Jim cannot depend on tourists or casual traffic. He must make sure his farm is a destination. He devises his activities for visitors carefully, with an eye on the costs. He cites his petting zoo as an example. At first, he was amused by the animals, and appreciated his visitors' pleasure in them. Soon he realized that these animals were costly. He put out feeding vending machines, and now the animals make money for him as well as entertain his guests.

School groups come in busloads to the orchard. Jim has plotted out an extensive one-hour guided tour, including hayrides, watching the grading machines work, learning about pruning, ending with the children picking their own apple off the tree to eat. Of course, to run as many as fifteen tours a day through means he has to hire staff, and when Jim added up the expense, he realized he needed to charge for the tours. He discovered charging actually improved the operation. For one thing, the buses arrive on time, and he can keep things on schedule. Everyone seems more attentive and interested, treating the tours as education rather than casual entertainment. Jim is building a one-room schoolhouse so he can hire a teacher to continue apple education on the weekends. He sees this as involving parents, grandparents, and children, and by charging on the weekends, he will be able to pay for his extra staff.

Jim thinks he can attract a lot more tour business. He is investigating working with senior citizens, because he realizes that children are not the only ones who want to learn, and seniors have the leisure to come out and visit, plus they spend while they are at the store.

Education is an essential part of Jim's pricing strategy. One day, a visitor told him that she thought he sure had an easy job. All he had to do was wait for the apples to ripen on the trees and then sell them. She thought other farmers had a lot more work than he did. He was barely able to smile and nod politely. He realized he had to help city people understand how much work is involved in fruit production, and consequently appreciate why his apples are expensive. He realized he could charge for his apples what the supermarkets did. The people who came to see the orchard really did not care what the prices were, they came for the experience.

Most people, that is. If Jim ever notices anyone who seems unhappy about the prices, he always goes up and gives them an apple. He tells his customers that no one is allowed to leave without an apple, and then he talks to them about apple farming, telling them about the process and answering their questions. He feels it is critical they understand his business, and why he charges the prices he does. When he is giving tours, he makes sure to point out his $30,000 tractor, as well as other costs he has so people realize the price of farming.

Jim is considering putting in a full-time bakery. Right now, he is working with neighbors to sell a few baked goods as an experiment. But he does not want to expand his hours. He feels that having the farm open only certain months gives it a special quality that he wants to preserve. His marketing niche attracts people who want a unique farm experience, not a supermarket trip. When children pick out a pumpkin, they get an adoption certificate, making the experience more than lifting something off the shelf.

Jim never forgets the importance of marketing. During a phone conversation, he mentioned he was waiting to hear back from television stations about an April Fools' Day hoax in which he was going to demonstrate how apple pies grow on trees, and how to carve a face on a pumpkin seed so your pumpkins come up all ready for Halloween.

Louise Hyde, Well-Sweep Farm, Port Murray, New Jersey

Louise and Cyrus Hyde started selling herb plants and dried flowers because he had grown up on a farm that had been in his family 200 years. Medicinal plants had always been a part of his family heritage.

Well-Sweep Farm began when Cy worked at a historical village, lecturing about uses of herbs. The tourists wanted to buy herb plants after seeing the gardens and hearing the lectures, so the Hydes bought four and a half acres to raise a few plants. Some time later, Louise delivered an ultimatum to her husband that he either quit his job and help with the business, or she was quitting as a wife.

Now they farm on 120 acres. Their greenhouses are filled with a collection of herb plants, including seventy different varieties of rosemary and thirty varieties of thyme. Demonstration gardens, educational displays, and a gift shop that sells herb books are part of the package. They host garden tours, lectures, cooking classes, and bus tours. They grow organically, but they have chosen not to be certified because of the paperwork. Louise feels that in their business it has not made much of a difference.

The retail business centers around a store that

sells herb plants and dried flowers. So many people are now offering dried flowers that Louise wants to focus more on herb sales. To bring people to the farm, every spring they have a festival featuring local craftspeople demonstrating and selling their crafts, guided lecture tours of the gardens, and lunch prepared by a local church group. Customers come in droves to buy their herbs for the summer season. Besides the spring festival, customers show up for a mid-season and fall harvest festival. Louise does little advertising; her retail store business has grown largely by word of mouth and the credibility from being in business for twenty-six years.

Louise does a large mail order business; every year she sends out 17,000 brochures. They ship live plants, generally dye plants and medicinal herbs, as well as topiary supplies, dried topiaries, and wreaths.

There are ways for the business to expand, but health department codes have restricted some of the options. Although Louise would like to produce herbal vinegars, strict New Jersey laws make a code kitchen a necessity, so at the moment she must retail other vinegars, at a price she feels is too expensive.

Louise recommends that people start small, with careful attention to keeping costs low. She sees the market expanding because more and more people are using herbs, and the interest in medicinal herbs is intensifying. People are eager to learn about herbs, so classes on medicinal uses, growing practices, and culinary uses are great sellers.

Dru Rivers, Full Belly Farm, Guinda, California

Dru Rivers, Paul Muller, Judith Redmond, and Raoul Adamchak have a farm in Northern California that has been certified organic for the last eight years. Their colorful booth is a welcome sight at farmers' markets throughout the Bay Area.

Dru, speaking for the farm, says that they are at a critical point. They cannot grow enough produce to meet the demand. If they could grow three times as much, they could sell it, but they are not sure they want to put that much pressure on themselves and their land.

Full Belly's success has been building slowly. Paul had grown up on a dairy farm, and Dru traveled all over the world working on farms. The two couples met while working and going to school at the University of California at Davis. Dru and Paul started the farm and Judith and Raoul joined them five years later.

They wholesale to specialty grocery and health food stores and sell at farmers' markets three times a week. They have started a community sustained agriculture program, delivering 180 boxes of vegetables to two drop points in the Bay Area once a week. This new program has received an overwhelming response. Even with dropouts, they have a list of subscribers waiting to participate. Currently, subscribers pay by the month, but the four partners hope to enlist people for a longer time period. In winter, when the weather makes selling at outdoor farmers' markets risky, the steady income and the knowledge that the crop is sold takes the worry out of farming.

Dru loves selling at farmers' markets, even though it means a twelve-hour day and too much driving in traffic. She and her partners work hard to make their booth attractive and to stand out. They sell the carded fleece from their sheep at the market stall; the rich blacks, browns, and grays always bring comment and customers. Flowers, wreaths, and gourds are all conversation pieces that attract strollers and make selling interesting. Dru says they try to have one of the owners at the market every time because they notice that sales increase when the owners are there. They also grow lots of unusual—Dru does not mince words; she calls them "weird"—greens, and people stop to buy and ask how to prepare them.

They have hosted a festival at the farm every summer called "Hoes Down," and it draws visitors from all over California. At first, Dru organized it to bring people to buy her dried flower wreaths. Then other people got involved, and now Hoes Down is a country festival with crafts, music, food, and lots of fun. Dru feels it is a particularly effective way to meet their customers, and she ascribes their loyalty to their seeing the farm during the festival.

The Full Belly crop system is extensive, producing about sixty different crops a year. Attention goes to building and maintaining a healthy, rich soil organically. In fact, Dru thinks that soil is essential to their success: customers say their vegetables taste better than other farms'.

Pam Montgomery, Green Terrestrial, Milton, New York

Pam is one of today's growers who became interested in herbs, and decided that she would change her life to accommodate her passion.

Seven acres of herb gardens in the Hudson River Valley produce the ingredients for medicinal teas and alcohol tinctures. Pam is also a wildcrafter, harvesting wild herbs from fields and forests near the farm to put into her blends. She has built a thriving business from herbs, and like all enthusiasts, she encourages others to try to imitate her success.

Pam got into the business because she trained with the noted herbalist Susan Weed, and people began to request weed walks with Pam to learn about beneficial plants. Then her students asked how to find the plants they saw on the walks and how to learn more about medicinal herbs. Now much of Pam's time is spent traveling around America lecturing on herbs and giving national workshops. She sees a growing interest in medicinal herbs linked to the interest in alternative medicines.

In 1992 she put up a building to house the business, hired a full-time assistant, and ordered a computer. She laughs about the journey from enjoying a hobby to running a full-time business. She recognizes the need for a business plan with specific goals to cover her monthly bills and overhead. As a first step, Pam has started to sell to wholesalers. She feels they will be a source of reliable income to help her stabilize her cash flow. Before, her business style concentrated on delivering personal service to individuals through mail order. Now her mailings reach 4,000 people and the list grows every month.

As a sideline, Pam raises herbs and vegetables for the Culinary Institute of America, a cooking school in Hyde Park, New York. She has used this reliable source of income to cover her costs while she builds her medicinal herb business.

Pam is excited about the future. Her business is expanding, and she feels confident in continued growth. She believes in the important resources for healing that alternative medicine practices offer. She feels there is a need for other people to grow medicinal herbs, and she hopes farmers will study the opportunities and try growing herbs as a business.

She grows organically, but she has not yet been certified organic. The complexity of the registration has put her off, but she hopes to begin work on certification soon. There are not enough growers producing organic herbs to match demand, and companies are forced to import herbs from countries with uncertain growing standards. Pam recommends placing ads in herb magazines or checking with the national herb associations for guidance on herb growing. The more growers the better, she suggests, because the more people who know about herbs, the more who will use them.

Cindy Nelson, City Worms and Compost, San Francisco

Another example of following your interest and making money from it is a gardener who grew up on a walnut grove in Stockton, California.

In 1992, while living in San Francisco, Cindy Nelson went through the master composting program of Alameda County run by the Cooperative Extension Service. As a newly credentialed teacher, she wanted to work as an environmental educator, teaching teachers about composting. As a part of the program, she owed a number of volunteer hours to pay for her training and so she wrote up a teachers' resource guide to composting. Quickly, Cindy found herself deluged with calls for more information about compost bins and yard waste boxes.

Cindy now sells worm and waste compost boxes made from plywood and ships live worms. She chose wood for the boxes because she feels strongly that petroleum products (plastics) are a nonrenewable resource, and that people needed the option to purchase a wood product. Cindy cuts out the boxes, puts them together, and ships them to her customers. She also offers a yard waste bin that makes turning the compost easy. She grows backyard worms in raised beds that used to hold her vegetables, but as demand increases, she finds she needs to expand her growing room to keep up with her customers' needs. Recently, she sold 30,000 worms in a week, and had to buy more worms from a worm farmer in Petaluma, California.

She spends lots of time talking to her customers about how to compost with worms. Properly done, the process yields superb, worm casting-rich compost for the back garden, without flies or odor.

Marketing for Cindy has been primarily word of mouth, with customers referring friends to her on a daily basis. She also teaches classes and passes out a simple, inexpensive brochure to her students. The master composting program also distributes brochures to its students. Cindy donates boxes to Bay Area demonstration gardens, and she takes every opportunity to teach classes.

Cindy is passionate about the ecological necessity for composting, and her goal is to encourage more households to get involved in trying to compost, both with vegetable scraps from their kitchens, and leaves and clippings from their yards and gardens. She encourages other people in the business, sharing her experiences and making suggestions. Cindy is convinced that the more people selling composting implements, the better business will become because it will make more and more people in the city aware of their choices.

The business has just started to get to a point where the weekends are not long enough to put together the boxes and tend to the worms. So far, Cindy has not made a profit, but that is because she is putting every penny she makes back into the business. She is looking into expanding her production by combining with a nonprofit organization, putting people to work and increasing the amount of customers she can handle.

As you can see from these stories, success involves a lot of hard work, but these experts are convinced that anyone can achieve it. Uniformly, they recommend starting small. They advise you to listen to your customers and take their suggestions. Quality and service are the two watchwords that these farmers say have made the difference in their businesses. Finally, these people are doing what they want to be doing, and if for you that means farming and growing quality products, well, you are bound to succeed.

CHAPTER 11

Old-Fashioned Farm Thrift

A farmer makes money when expenses run less than income, and as easy and as self-evident as that may seem, the reality of thrifty farming is a lot more difficult. A spate of mechanical problems, the ravages of mother nature, or simple bad luck can send you to the bank for a loan when you're out of money before the end of the month. There are a number of books available that suggest ways to increase income through shrewd and clever marketing tactics, but not as many include suggestions on how to decrease costs. This is unfortunate, considering cost-cutting is as much a part of a successful farm operation as increasing income.

Before World War II, farmers on small, diversified farms rarely went to the store because their farms produced and recycled everything they needed. With the introduction of mechanical tractors and the change in farming systems to monoculture production, farms became more dependent on making money from one crop and spending the earnings to pay for the other things the farm no longer produced. As farmers no longer used animals in the production system, they purchased synthetic fertilizers to maintain the fertility of their fields. Buying and maintaining tractors, plus the fuel costs to run them for hours every day added to farmers' mounting expenses, so regular infusions of cash became necessary. Consequently, many farmers are taking a new look at their production systems as costs continue to climb and income from agricultural products tends to stay about the same. They are reexamining the concepts of diversified farming, not only to increase profits, but also to decrease expenses.

Other than land taxes, electricity, and wages for farm labor, costs come mainly from inputs—from seeds, to fertilizers, to feed. Gasoline and oil, water when the well runs out, fertilizers for the fields, and feed or bales of hay for the animals can add up to an astonishing monthly total expense. You may find you spend more money taking care of your animals, land, and machines than your family. If you can lessen the costs of inputs through a more efficient integration of your farm system, while saving money on equipment and tools, your bottom line will increase. Animals figure into this equation as manufacturers of fertilizer while providing mowing services. If well managed, they can be money savers as well as money makers, providing a cash crop of meat or livestock, or byproducts of fleece and milk.

Besides the practical aspect of cutting costs, there is also a philosophical aspect. Many farmers are looking closely at a newly titled system— although it has all the same characteristics of pre-1940's diversified farming—called biodynamic farming, which they find both practical and monetarily rewarding. The biodynamic system looks at the fertility of the soil to design farming systems that mimic the natural processes, which in turn increase tilth and sustainability. By using a rotational system of animals and cover crops that naturally fertilize the soil, the farmers find they can combine animals and crop production in a manner that efficiently uses time and money while lessening inputs.

Not every farm situation encourages the addition of farm animals; however, there are other ways, equally old-fashioned, that can help you balance your costs against your income.

Pay for What You Buy in Cash

For new farmers or farmers starting up a sideline farm business, whether a dairy farmer planting grapes or a berry farmer adding a line of jams, brand new equipment can be an expense that takes years to earn out. Rushing out to buy exactly what you need to get the job done may make you feel deligent and efficient—your time is worth money of course—and when you are in the middle of starting up your operation, it may seem much easier to put purchases on a credit card just to get going. However, these tendencies are as dangerous to your project budget as throwing money out an open window. If you fall behind on your monthly payments, you will add the high interest of borrowed money to your overhead.

So, don't squander your money; there are economical tactics every farmer can use. Plan to pay in cash, buy "new-to-you" equipment, and look for ways to barter (not buy) to save money in the beginning. Avoiding the credit card crunch is one of the best money-saving tactics you can employ to put your farm on a sound financial basis. When you go to town, leave your credit cards at home.

Planning is another money-saving tactic. A written farm plan works most efficiently through an entire farming career. In the beginning, take the time to sit down and plan. Though it may seem unimportant compared to planting, cleaning barns, or talking to customers, it is important to make a start, even with just a simple idea. Start by comparing available cash to your estimated monthly expenses (See page 75). When you need to buy equipment, compare prices for different models and different years. Some tractors, such as John Deere, have the name recognition that makes them more expensive than others, such as Fords. Make sure you know what job you need to do with each piece of equipment; for example, buying an inexpensive tractor without a front bucket may mean you will need to buy another tractor down the line if you plan on moving piles of manure instead of just spreading it. When you shop around, jot down estimated costs so that you can accurately plan to make your purchase when cash is available to you. Once you know relative prices you can also consider your other options, such as renting for quick jobs and buying older equipment from another farmer.

Get to Know Your Neighbors

One way to save money on equipment is to share equipment owned by your neighbors, either by renting it or persuading them to do the job for you. The form of persuasion can be barter, cash, or goodwill. Getting to know your neighbors may be one of the most money-saving efforts you can make.

In most areas, farmers are still neighborly, and becoming a good neighbor can not only bring you the pleasures of community and friendship, but economic savings as well. Farm neighbors are used to pitching in to help out one another, whether simply sharing a cup of coffee, or lending a strong back or their backhoe. It may take a while to get to know your neighbors, but make every effort. Wave when walking the fences or stop by to drop off extra produce. Good neighbor relations can bring you help when you need it most.

City folk, newly come to the country, may think they should not intrude into the privacy of their neighbors, but remember, in most places outside the city limits and outside of city services, neighbors need to provide assistance to one another. You will be expected to stop by and introduce yourself, and those who don't—because they don't understand the local customs—may seem standoffish.

Your neighbors are one of your most valuable resources for free advice and assistance. Usually, however, they wait for you to ask their opinion, not volunteering until they have gotten to know you. Farmers cannot afford the expense or the time of calling a plumber every time a pipe breaks, ringing up the electrician when a light switch doesn't work, or hiring someone to do fairly simple repairs. Growing up on a farm still means learning how to be a mechanic, welder, electrician, plumber, veterinarian, carpenter, cook, and bottle washer. Most farmers are willing to share their valuable skills with a beginner who needs help, and after a few times you will know what to do for yourself. Of course, there are times when you must resort to the professionals and pay the price, but many farmers have saved the bill from the well maintenance company by checking the fuses or jiggling the breakers to get the well going after a power outage.

Asking for assistance instead of calling for the repairman builds a bond between neighbors that can lead to trading labor, from fencing to ditch clearing. Of course, in the beginning, you can offer to hire a neighbor if they are using a tractor or large piece of equipment. Because many services start billing from the time the truck leaves the yard, hiring neighbors still saves money on transportation costs. Look for low-cost courses in the community colleges or adult-education schools to help round out your skills and make you as self-sufficient as possible.

Old-time farmers are not stingy or miserly; however, they are cautious. They hate to spend their money and respect others with the same philosophy. Barter for what you need, offering something they want. Cattle raisers may consider trading a young motherless calf for a butchered lamb or grazing rights on land not being used. Everyone always needs extra help, so offering to trade labor may provide you with extra, free help when you need it most.

Lastly, many companies in farm areas rent equipment for inexpensive daily sums, which include delivery and pick-up. Specialized equipment, from small tractors to manure spreaders and stump grinders can be rented and returned for a fraction of the cost of purchase. Plus, there is no worry about maintaining and storing them for the rest of the year.

Don't forget the fountain of free wisdom and experience available from your local farm agent. Linked to the state university system, farm agents can provide you with free or inexpensive pamphlets as well as offer a variety of classes, seminars, and farm visits that advise you of the latest farm methods, products, and market information. Working with them links you to a network of other farmers in the area who can provide additional resources. For the computer literate, online services provide additional information in a number of different forums. (See Chapter 12).

Pinching Pennies

If you must buy a piece of equipment, try to purchase it used. Check the advertisements in the local papers under the farmer's column, look on bulletin boards in feed or ranch supply stores, and ask around for other local sources of used equipment. Some new farm equipment stores also have a used equipment yard. Don't neglect to ask all your neighbors; most farmers have outbuildings filled with equipment which they might be willing to sell. There is always the risk of buying something that proves to be worn out and useless, but researching the types of equipment available will give you an idea of what can successfully be repaired. Call the local tractor store, talk with your farm agent, and check the library to unearth models known to be reliable.

Barn sales, garage sales, and auctions sell items so cheaply it is astounding. Though you spend valuable time, in the off-season you can dig up good tools at inexpensive prices. Fine quality shovels that usually sell in hardware stores for twelve to thirty dollars can be found at bargain stores for fifty cents. Many of the older tools are not only less expensive when bought at these sales, they also have been made from better materials than those currently produced, and with proper care, will outlast you. Electrical equipment, plumbing pipe, hacksaws, and glue, can be bought for pennies at sales, lumped together, in dusty boxes. Of course, organizing these different items so you know what you have when you need it is critical, but clipboards with items sorted in categories such as electrical, plumbing, and carpentry can help you remember your inventory.

Look also for used items to serve in new ways. Inexpensive plastic PVC pipe can be formed into structures for greenhouses from large walk-in buildings to row covers. Battered bathtubs make fine water troughs for sheep, horses, and cows. Old fence wire can be made into circles for compost or vertical towers for vining produce such as tomatoes, cucumbers, and beans. One thrifty farmer made a chicken coop by simply covering a rusty, metal lumber rack with wire.

Of course, you can be penny wise and pound foolish, meaning there are times when you must spend the money to buy a piece of equipment that does exactly the job you need it to do. Experience will teach you what you need to spend money on versus corners you can profitably cut. Budgeting for the bigger ticket items, and saving on the myriad of smaller items can equip your tool room quickly and cheaply.

INTEGRATING LIVESTOCK INTO THE FARM OPERATION TO LESSEN INPUT COSTS

The cost of fertilizers continues to climb, but adding animals to your farm system can help diminish those costs. According to Jerome D. Belanger in his book *The Homesteader's Handbook to Raising Small Livestock*, a ton of sheep manure contains 28 pounds of nitrogen and 20 pounds of phosphorus. Cows produce 15 pounds of nitrogen per ton, horses 13.8, dairy cows 11.2, and pigs 10. A beef cow will produce 8.5 tons of fertilizer for every 1,000 pounds of body weight.

Chickens and rabbits produce even higher amounts of nitrogen in their manure, so much that farmers need to use caution when applying fresh manure to avoid burning the plants. One doe and her 28 babies (based on 4 litters per year) produce an estimated 168 pounds of high nitrogen fertilizer (enough to spread over an 84-square-foot garden). Composting this high nitrogen manure before applying it is more successful than applying it fresh.

Based on these figures, you can see that it makes a lot of sense—and cents—to include animals in your operation, but, it must be said at the outset, in many situations, animals may not be appropriate at all. The idea of "virtually" free fertilizer, food, and farm charm must be instantly discarded, as anyone who has kept animals knows. Absolutely nothing about animals is free. Animals eat all year round regardless of what is out in the pasture; they get sick all year long, with resulting vet and medication bills; and they make you pay close attention to your fences, to avoid escapes onto the road or into a neighbor's field, which can result in a liability situation. Still, if well integrated into your farm systems, livestock can help you run your business more efficiently by providing fertilizer and food, and if you like animals, they are a pleasure to view on the land and delightful companions.

Until the mid 1940s, when gas-driven tractors

became the primary source of energy on the farm, most everyone kept animals in an integrated farm system. With the changing economics, a diversified farm that provided a small amount of cash, but sustained a family with food and housing, changed to a monoculture production system. These farmers specialized in crops such as wheat production, milk production, or all beef production. Suddenly old MacDonald's farm faded into distant history. Pesticides and farm subsidies dealt the final blow, and farm families began to buy their milk, eggs, and vegetables at the grocery store. Yet, as our ancestors knew when they took the time to tame wild animals and breed them into beasts of burden, animals can save the farmer time and money while adding income to the farm.

Yet animals can mean veterinary bills, feed bills, housing expenses, and usually a dash of aggravation, so preplanning is essential to work them into your production schedule. Consult with your farm agent about your land and the most efficient, inexpensive birds or animals to compliment your system. Weeder geese are great in orchards, as are pigs, to keep them clean of weeds or fallen fruit. Chickens in movable coops, while requiring little feed, can be transported around a cattle pasture to break up the cow pies, eat out the fly maggots, and provide high nitrogen fertilizer and fresh eggs. In Washington State, Canterbury Farms raises horses and uses the composted stable droppings and cedar chips to mulch their blueberries. This works well because the berries relish in the high-acid mixture so freely produced by the horses. In Brentwood, California, a farmer uses the weeder geese in his apricot orchard to keep down grasses. Sheep produce a fertilizer high in phosphorus, making the fertiliz-

er perfect for growing lettuce greens and bromeli-
ads. At the same time, sheep are superb lawn
mowers, as they browse along fence lines efficiently, munching down weeds and grass in non-
productive areas.

Once you have decided to add animals to your
system, look for a community college course or
work with a neighbor or friend to learn how to
handle the animals you plan to buy. Choosing the
right breed for the task is essential. If you want
sheep for the dual purpose of food and fiber,
choosing a breed that produces fiber and meat
makes better sense than choosing the standard
meat lamb which produces only a mediocre short-
stapled wool. Some cow breeds can be milked
while others are used solely for meat production.
A light chicken such as a leghorn, produces eggs
regularly and can be slaughtered for chicken
stock, but it is too bony to provide a fried chick-
en dinner.

Don't accept any free animals until you know
the real cost. A goose might turn into a raging, territorial dragon that intimidates children, bites,
attacks, and spreads slimy-slick manure everywhere it goes. A cantankerous cow, kindly given
to you by a good friend, may break into the garden—they instinctively lean on shaky fences—
and eat up a whole summer's menu in about fifteen minutes. A goat that looks healthy on the
outside may bring intestinal worms into your pastures and infect the rest of your herd. Free dogs
that haven't been raised on a farm may take
extreme patience and temper to train. If not well-
trained, dogs may chase and kill your animals, as
well as those of the neighbors', all of which you
will have to pay for. Interrupting your work constantly to discipline an animal can be both frus-

trating and a waste of production time.

Quarantine all new farm animals for at least a week to make sure they are healthy and will not infect your other animals with a disease or parasite problems. Cows, sheep, and goats are prone to wasting diseases, foot rot, and parasites that will infect your soil and become a problem for your existing herd. The prices of animals at auctions are tempting, but when you calculate the hidden costs from undiagnosed health problems, you may choose to buy from reliable breeders, after checking out their references. Most reputable breeders stand by their stock, so if a problem arises within a reasonable amount of time, the breeder will take the animal back or refund your money.

Balance the added cost of a purebred pedigree with the purpose you plan for the animals. Crossbred animals can be bought more cheaply than pure-bred animals and though they won't make a difference in terms of sales price for meat, they sell for much less as breeding stock.

Keep good records because as in any business venture, you need to know just what the costs are to figure the income. Knowing the feed and vet costs as well as their seasonal rise and fall, will help you fine tune your system. Don't forget that you will need to cull animals and sell off the ones that eat but don't produce income. Keeping old Flossy around because she looks nice in the field even though she no longer produces, is fine for one animal who has served you well in the past, but if you are running a retirement village for seniors, you will lose money. Because there is a huge gap between sentimentality and factory animal farming, the diversified farmer needs to be realistic, not just romantic, to keep the animal husbandry on a sound financial basis. If you want to make money from your animals, both in measured cash income and in reduction of inputs, you'll know by studying your records whether you have a cash flow or a cash hemorrhage.

Lastly, if you are new to working with animals, start to build your numbers slowly. It takes some time to become familiar with handling animals so that at a glance you can tell a sick animal from a healthy one, anticipate problems with fields and fences, and provide adequate housing and food. All animals add a burden of routine and responsibility to keep them fed, bred, and healthy, severely limiting your time away from the farm. Also, there are hidden costs on your time even if you do profit from them in food or cash returns. For example, those lovely ewes that serve as such great lawn and field mowers during the summer transform your life into a state of constant exhaustion during lambing season. Getting up several times a night to check on potential new mothers is quite tiring when you are also working a day job or running a vegetable production farm. The ewes must also be rounded up several times a year to have their hooves trimmed and fleece sheared. Too many animals can put your whole farm out of whack with excessive demands of time and money. Be cautious and start slow.

These following brief overviews of different animals will help you consider your options and decide whether specific animals can benefit your farm operation and finances. Extensive literature is available on any of the following creatures if you decide to add them to your farm. If possible, read up on the other animals, visit other farms, and speak to your farm advisor.

Poultry and Exotic Birds

Every farm used to have the traditional crowing roosters and contentedly clucking hens, ducks and geese to provide eggs, meat, and fertilizer. The term "egg money" once referred to the sale of eggs to bring in enough extra money for a few special treats for the farm family. Now, with the price of eggs from free-range chickens almost double that of store-bought eggs, the term "egg money" can mean enough monthly income to pay off feed bills for the other animals, plus food for your own refrigerator and fertilizer for the farm.

The most successful small-egg operations build flocks of different varieties of free-range chickens that supply multi-colored and multi-sized eggs in one carton. These eggs, when marketed under the consumer-favorite labels of "free-range and fertile," can bring as much as double the price (or more) per carton than grocery store prices of equally-sized white or brown eggs. Quail eggs have special market appeal for caterers and restaurants, bringing much higher prices than their size would attest.

Poultry can be housed in small spaces, requiring only minimal time for feeding and maintenance. If kept clean and dry, they usually stay healthy and deliver high-nitrogen fertilizer to replace purchased fertilizer; however, they must be fed year-round for egg production, so be sure to factor in the cost of feed and housing when planning a poultry venture.

There are ways to minimize the amount of feed they need. Chickens in movable houses pretty much feed themselves during clement weather when transferred from location to location in a field or orchard Chickens also sort through and scatter dung, which reduces flies and breaks up the manure, allowing it to decompose more quickly when exposed to rain. Turning them out into a cover crop just before you plow gives them lots of fresh feed, plus they leave behind the benefit of their high-nitrogen fertilizer. Storing them overnight in a field in a wire-bottomed coop, spreads the manure without any work for the farmer.

Predators can be a problem, decimating your flock. Secure cages are essential in housing any poultry because skunks, raccoons, and foxes consider chickens prime targets. The poultry house should be encased in wire, including the bottom, if possible for protection at night. Check the perimeters often for signs of burrowing; loose neighborhood dogs can make short work of a flock during the daytime.

Exotic birds, such as quail and pheasant can be raised for the restaurant market under certified conditions; however, pigeons have some disadvantages as they carry diseases which may infect humans. Raising birds for the pet market such as canaries, parakeets, finches, and parrots may also be quite lucrative, but before you jump into a breeding program, take time to investigate the legal requirements and regulations governing these birds.

Ducks and geese may also be allowed to range, feeding themselves and providing free grazing and bug disposal. Some farmers in areas with invasions of locusts and grasshoppers or slugs and snails, encircle their production areas with a wired-in ring of ducks. Waddling the ring, the ducks voraciously gobble up the pests. Though younger ducks are usually better at this than their elders, Indian Runner ducks have the reputation of maintaining their appetites even as adults.

Weeder geese may also be beneficial in production areas, as they keep an orchard nicely weeded and grazed without damaging the trees. Neither ducks nor geese must have a pond to swim in, but a constant supply of fresh drinking water is required.

Most poultry can be purchased in the local feed stores or through catalogs as hatchlings, but shipping is limited to spring, summer, and early fall to protect the health of the delicate babies. Check your local newspapers to purchase adult birds.

Rabbits

Rabbits on the farm provide both food and manure, but there is little or no market for the skins; although, if you have the time and will to hand-comb the fur of the angora rabbits, it sells for good prices. Slaughtering for resale must be done according to the regulations of the local health department, but is simple for home use. Prepared like chicken, rabbit meat is quite delicious. The manure is high in nitrogen and easily gathered to be composted and spread.

Although there are systems to run rabbits on the ground in colonies, most farmers keep them in wire cages, feeding them processed alfalfa pellets that provide the necessary nutrition; supplementing with hay and vegetables is also advisable. Alfalfa hay, leguminous cover crops, carrots, and comfrey (*Symphytum officinale*) are superior additions to the rabbits' diets that can lessen the amount of pelleted foods you feed them.

One doe can produce at least thirty babies a year, providing more food per pound than any other farm animal. Does have a gestation period of

31 days, and are bred as often as every eight to ten weeks, although some breeders have an even more intensive schedule. Most of the rabbits used for meat are the California Whites with pink eyes, or the New Zealands with brown eyes. Both are large rabbits that gain weight well and are economical producers in terms of feed/weight ratios.

Don't forget the lucrative pet market for some of the smaller breeds as well as the laboratory market. Again, check out the demand before you start your breeding program.

Cows, Sheep, and Goats

These larger farm animals are called ruminants, because of their multiple stomachs that allow them to digest grass and hay. They generate a by-product of manure that returns fertility to the soil. Their grazing habits are the subject of hotly-contested debates between environmentalists and large-scale graziers. Side-stepping that controversy, let it be said that for the small farmer, with attention to grazing practices, these animals improve pastures. With management, these four-legged mowers can clean out a field for you while spreading seeds (in the manure) and fertilizer.

A system of limited grazing with rotation through small paddocks has become the subject of much interest and practice. Highly intensive grazing, through confinement with electric or stationary fencing, keeps the animals on a limited patch of pasture for a few hours or days. This system allows the pasture to be grazed evenly, and to grow back before the animals return to graze again. The system works with the grazing habits of the animals that browse the field, first eating the favored food, then the less desirable food. If allowed to stay for long periods of time in a field, the animal continually returns to the favored food, finally killing it as it eats below the crown, denuding a pasture. This may be avoided by moving the animals after their first grazing, allowing the pasture grasses to regrow. More time between grazing on a piece of land inhibits worm and parasite infestation. Understanding these principles helps many farmers raise more animals on a smaller section of land, as well as improve the animals' health and lessen dependence on worming compounds.

Besides the useful addition of four-legged manure spreaders, other small industries associated with these animals can add to your income base. There is a growing cottage industry of handcrafted cheeses that bring premium prices in specialty stores and through catalog sales. Cow, sheep, and goat's milk cheeses have a growing appreciative audience willing to pay high prices for fine flavors. Groups such as the American Cheese Society have encouraged and spread a good reputation for small producers. Books, classes, and annual conferences on cheese and its production can help you get started in this venture. Organic dairy products bring premium prices because there are few producers in the marketplace.

Although more limited in marketability, fleece of fine quality does sell well to weavers, handspinners, and craftspeople. There is growing interest in domestic cashmere and mohair production, and these groups have magazines and support associations that provide assistance. Your farm agent can put you in touch with these sources, or you can contact them through the

Internet.

Historic farm museums and other living history groups are interested in purchasing domestic animals of minor breeds (old-fashioned breeds now out of commercial production and often facing extinction). These animals can be located across the country through the individual breed association or through American Minor Breeds, but their cost is often inflated due to the limited supply of animals. The prices of exotic animals such as llamas and vicunas have plunged recently, although there is still interest. Should you wish to invest in these animals, study this volatile market closely.

Lastly, don't forget that farms with on-site sales or activities benefit from petting zoos or just the scenic attraction of grazing animals. These farms could potentially become a field trip destination for families, senior tour groups, and schools. (See Chapter 7).

Bringing animals back to the farm can save you time and money; however, they should pay their way, not add to your burden of expense. Although farmers are often discounted when they wax sentimental about the beauty and serenity of animals, they aren't always wrong. If you know you are saving on inputs and making money with your animals, you really will feel serene. In fact, the cluck of the chicken as she lays an egg may become music to your ears.

Although the saying is "it takes money to make money," assessing or reassessing your farm operation to save money pays off as well. Making more and more money doesn't help you if you increase your spending at the same time. Tightening up your spending—just as the old thrifty-minded farmers once did—can make your operation a success.

Resources

American Cheese Society
c/o Laura Jacobs Welch
P.O. Box 303
Delavan, WI 53115
262/728-4458
www.cheesesociety.org

Countryside Magazine, W 11564 Highway 64, Withee, WI 54498

Calling itself the magazine for homesteaders, this magazine requires you to wade through a number of personal testimonies, but serves as a fine compendium of useful moneysaving ideas and lots of practical, thrifty information.

The Contrary Farmer, Gene Logsdon, Chelsea Green Publishing Company,
P.O. Box 130, Route 113, Post Mills, VT 05058

A book filled with practical ideas from a real farmer who also writes passionately and humorously about diversified farming–from buying tractors to anecdotes about the painter Andrew Wyeth. An enjoyable read for city slicker and farmer alike.

CHAPTER 12

Obtaining Helpful Sources through the Internet

Although many of us would rather walk fences than surf the Internet, only the stick-in-the-muds refuse to recognize the incredible convenience of accessing crop information, detailed weather and temperature analysis, farming, and marketing information from their own homes. Of course, learning to use the system at first is overwhelming—there are hundreds of different choices for information—but like any task, after the first few feeble tries, you become an old hand. Try to have a friend act as guru to get you started. Choose someone who's willing to answer your questions and receive querulous phone calls night or day. After the first several times, you won't need to call your friend, you can ask your pals through e-mail.

There are two different functions that you can use "online." The Internet is a communication service that uses electronic mail to let people send notes, memos, and queries to each other all over the world. There are also discussion groups that use e-mail when working on projects to discuss particular issues, or keep up-to-date on the newest research. Then there is the Web, which is an information sharing service. Although there is now a great deal of advertising on the Web, with a small amount of work you can find Web sites that link you to libraries such as the USDA or large university agricultural libraries, print magazines from *Organic Gardening* to the *New York Times*, and thousands of newsletters on technical subjects.

To participate, you need a phone, a computer, a modem and an Internet service. These services charge you a flat monthly rate for an unlimited number of hours. When using electronic mail, write your notes first and then click on the Internet to send them, so you use little phone time. If you are searching the Web, you may use more time but you can copy any pertinent information you find onto your hard disk for later reading or printing out, also saving net time. Your phone will be in use while you are on the Internet or the Web, so if you need a phone available at all times, you must bring in a second line, called a dedicated line, for your electronic adventures.

Due to the unprecedented success of the Internet, there are now many services offering a host of different features at different prices. Shop around for the best local company for your planned uses. Look at the amount of time they offer as a part of the flat fee, and if you think you need international service, ask how they charge for that. Some allow you to browse Italian newspapers, should you wish, as long as you want, for no additional fee, while others are limited to national boundaries. With some services you need a special software program to access the Internet and a research vehicle or browser to scan the Web. Sometimes they are given away free by the Internet service, or included in the service so as soon as you are hooked up, you are ready to go.

Each information site on the Web has an address—a series of letters, dots, slashes, and colons—that direct you there. When you connect, the first thing you see is a home page, a kind of table of contents to the resources of that site. The particular magic of the Web is that many sites are linked to other information sources, so when you are at one site and click the mouse on highlighted words to investigate a particular topic, the Web links you automatically with another information source that can exhaustively discuss that issue, without you even knowing it. Using bookmarks, you record which sites you have visited and where you have found useful information so you can find your way back. With a click of your electronic wand, libraries full of information, lists of farmers markets, packets of "how to" on CSA's, and tips and techniques for organic farming and gardening appear on your screen to be downloaded to your computer so you can read them over at your leisure. Other sites offer marketing opportunities to help you find buyers for your products. It is a mind-boggling, unlimited resource for sharing information and keeping yourself up-to-date on the latest techniques, crops, and resources.

An easy starting place for your agricultural research is the Small Farm Center of the University of California, Davis. They offer the latest research, ranging from a pest section relating to deer and gophers to crop information on maple syrup, garlic, and hay, among others. Besides their own pieces, they link to other sites for further research. They also offer a listing of other Web sites with useful offerings. If you have questions or suggestions, they have an e-mail address for correspondence.

E-mail is a lively source of information, anecdotes, suggestions, and off-the-wall tactics.
Because the information provided through e-mail
is from a variety of different sources it is not
always accurate; therefore, it is not endorsed by
the Web site, but encouraged for its potential
assistance. It comes with the warning to use it at
your own risk, but you may find it a source of
helpful information from others.

Besides providing a wealth of information from
individuals and universities, there are also marketing opportunities. Any individual can set up a
Web page providing information about crops or
products, from selling wool to informing CSA
members what produce is available. Many of us
who have shunned modern conveniences and
have chosen a simpler way of life have wished to
avoid joining this electronic movement; but, it is
just too useful to ignore any longer. Try it out at a
local library or community college and you cannot help but immediately want to continue to
access the information it provides. Don't worry
about becoming lost in the Web. When those
weeds start to grow, consult the Web for cover
crops that more effectively compete with weeds
next year. Then shut off the machine and go out to
work!

Resources

University of Florida Institute of Food and
Agricultural Sciences
http://www.ifas.ufl.edu/

Excellent compilation of web sites featuring
agricultural information.

@griculture Online
http://www.agriculture.com

Small Farm Center, University of California at Davis
http://www.sfc.ucdavis.edu/

A listing of online newsletters and publications,
calendar of conferences, other Web sites with
related information, and materials in Spanish.

Afterword

Growing things is magic. Nurturing backyard fruit trees or a whole orchard, working sweet soil under your hoe, and inhaling the perfume of a fine early morning bring a deep satisfaction that harks back through the history of humankind. Stewards of the land we continue to be, and the pleasures are real, even though tempered with long hours of backbreaking labor, swarms of grasshoppers, or clouds of mildew. As growers know, working the earth is in our blood, and we can recapture the meaning even if we have spent most of our lives working inside an office building. Whether you were born on the farm or have become a grower later in life, the rewards wait for everyone.

Joining the ranks of our ancestors who weeded, hoed, and chewed the edge of a grass sliver, we can enjoy the pleasures of raising food and sharing with others. Seed choices—made in the glow of lamplight to the howl of winter winds—reward us with green plants in summer's warmth. When you hand over your first lettuce to an eager customer, or sack up the first pound of tomatoes, you will remember the moment with a silent smile that belies worries over paying the feed bill, rebuilding the raised bed that collapsed the day before, or having the time to pick up the kids before you set the evening sprinklers.

You become part of a proud line of history by feeding people with fresh, wholesome, and nourishing food. As a revolutionary, as a pioneer, there are a number of hazards and unknowns before you. While you design your crop rotations, turn the compost, or call to find new customers, never forget you are certainly doing something urgently important.

Although the practice of growing food is as old as humankind, to revitalize America's food sources is to be part of a new consciousness that brings our values back to simple, real pleasures of the hearth. Good ingredients make good food, and good food is to be shared. In a time of industrial mechanization and individual isolation, sharing food with our friends, neighbors, and our families renews the spirit and brings people together in a very grand harvest indeed.

A Compendium of Wild and Useful Ideas

A lthough the Cornell University Farming Alternatives Program no longer updates this list or disseminates information about individual items, still it provides a mind-boggling list of interesting ideas to start any farmer thinking about new markets.

They do warn, in capital letters, that they make no claims as to the feasibility of any of these ideas. You may be surprised by the range of possibilities out there for you, but some of them are somewhat risky. Suggest ostrich farming in some circles and then duck, no pun intended!

Biotech Products and Products for Scientific Use

Blood products from animals, e.g., rabbits, chinchilla

Guinea pigs

Horse urine

Rabbits

Field Crops

Adzuki beans

Amaranth grain for food and feed

Barley

Birdseed (sunflowers, etc.)

Buckwheat

Canola for oil

Corn snack foods

Fresh or stone ground flours and grains

Fuel crops (ethanol generations, etc.)

Hard red spring wheat

Indian corn, miniature or regular sized

Jerusalem artichokes for cattle feed and human consumption

Lupines, sweet, as cash grain and for feed

Malting barley

Organically grown grains of all types

Popcorn, white and colored

Seed production

Soybeans for human consumption

Soybeans processed into tofu, tempeh food products

Sunflower for oil and birdseed

Wild rice

Fish and Game

Bait fish

Beefalo (hybrid of buffalo and cattle)

Bullhead catfish production with aquaculture techiques

Deer farming (production of venison for restaurant trade)

   Fallow deer

   Red deer

   Elk (wapiti)

Eels for export to Europe

Fish bait

Game farms for tourists

Guinea fowl

Mallard duck for meat

Peacocks for feathers

Pheasant rearing for release/restocking programs and for meat

Rabbits (Angora) for hair

Rabbits for meat

Salmon

Squab (young pigeon)

Trout

Forest Products

Apple tree firewood

Balsam pillows and wild herbs

Cedar oil

Christmas trees

Fiddleheads (unprotected species)

Firewood

Furniture (e.g., outdoor chairs and picnic tables)

Ginseng

Hemlock for pharmaceutical industry

Hybrid poplar for fuel

Locust for posts and pods for forage

Morel mushrooms

Nuts

Sawlogs

Shiitake mushrooms

Toys from wood

Tree seed collection

Willow for pharmaceutical industry

Fruits

Apples

Applesauce

Berry products: jams, jellies, wines, juices, pie fillings

Blackberries

Blueberries, highbush cultivated and lowbush foraged

Cider

Cranberries

Currants

Dried fruit

Elderberries, elderberry wine

Fruit leathers

Gooseberries

Grape juice, fresh white and pink

Grape pie filling

Kiwi, greenhouse culture of hardy varieties

Mixed berry juices

Mulberries

Raspberries: red, black, purple, and yellow

Strawberries, day neutral types

Table grapes, seeded and seedless

Wine grapes for home brewing

Horticultural/Nursery

Annual flowers sold as potted plants

Dried flowers, cultivated and wild

Field-grown cut flowers

Field-grown mums

Herb bedding plants, wholesale market

Herbs for culinary purposes

Herbs for potpourri and dried arrangements

Nasturtium flowers as edible salad ingredient

Northern hardy ornamental shrubs and perennial flowers, wholesale

Organically raised bedding plants and fruit trees

"Wild" local species cultivated, e.g., trillium and bloodroot

Livestock and Animals

Beef, conventional and organic or "chemical free"

Deer farming (for fine-grade venison)

  Fallow deer

  Red deer

Donkeys, miniature

Elk

Fox: silver, red, and blue

Goats (Angora) for hair

Goats for milk, cheese, and meat

Honey and beeswax products

Horses, trail rides, draft horse breeding

Llama for pack animals, hair, and pets

Mink

Rabbits (Angora) for hair

Rabbits for meat and lab animals

Sheep for lamb and mutton, wool, milk (for cheese)

Sheepskin leather products

Veal, conventional and certified

Poultry

Balut (duck eggs partially incubated)

Chicken eggs, partially developed, for Asian markets

Chicken processed into patties for wholesale markets

Ducks for liver pâté

Ducks for meat

Free-range poultry of all types

Geese

Organically raised poultry of all types

Squab (young pigeon)

Turkey: fresh, frozen, or cooked

Services and Recreation

Antique shop

Bed and breakfast inn

Boat storage

Bottle return center

Campground

Child care in country setting

Composting of municipal wastes

Custom machinery work

Custom planting and care of vegetables

Custom planting and care of window boxes and container annuals

Custom slaughter

Farm sitting

Festivals during peak harvest periods

Gift shops

Hunting, fishing, and nature hike guides

Lectures on herbs, gardening

Museum of old farm equipment on working farm

Pet motels for large as well as small animals

Petting zoo

Racehorse recuperation farms

Religious services, e.g., sunrise Easter services, weddings

Restaurant

Seed and supplies distributor

Sleigh rides with workhorses

Small engine repair

Taxidermy, mammal and bird

Tea services, catered at farm

Tours

Vacations on farm

Vegetables

Asian vegetables

Asparagus

Baby vegetables

Burdock root for macrobiotic market

Chutney sauces

Cole crops (broccoli, cauliflower, Brussels sprouts, kohlrabi)

Endive

Garlic

Gourmet vegetables

Horseradish

Hydroponically produced crops, out of season

Indian corn: regular, strawberry type, and mini-multicolored

Mushrooms: bisporous, shiitake, etc.

Onions (diversification, e.g., transplants, shallots, sweet, early)

Organic vegetables of all types

Peppers: green and specialty types (purple, hot, etc.)

Pesto (basil sauce)

Pumpkins

Sprouts from beans, mustards, etc.

Sweet potatoes

Tomatoes, specialty types

Vinegars, herb

Watercress and other water-produced vegetables

Crop Production Bibliography

A number of excellent resources are available to assist you in learning new production techniques. If you are confused by the terms *low-input, intercropping,* or *intensive planting,* these books will enlighten you.

Coleman, Eliot. *The New Organic Grower: A Master's Manual of Tool and Techniques for the Home and Market Gardener.* Chelsea, Vt.: Chelsea Green, 1989

Creasey, Rosalind. *Cooking from the Garden: Creative Gardening and Contemporary Cuisine.* San Francisco: Sierra Club Books, 1988.

Gibson, Eric. *Sell What You Sow: A Guide to Successful Produce Marketing.* Carmichael, Calif.: New World Publishing, 1994.

Jeavons, John. *How to Grow More Vegetables Than You Thought Possible on Less Land Than You Can Imagine.* Berkeley, Calif.: Ten Speed Press, 1991.

Lima, Patrick. *The Natural Food Garden: Growing Vegetables and Fruits Chemical-Free.* Rocklin, Calif.: Prima Publishing, 1992.

Specialty and Minor Crop Handbook. Small Farm Center Publications, University of California Davis, 1992.

This book is also available on disk.

Sturdivant, Lee. *Profits from Your Backyard Herb Garden.* 1988. San Juan Naturals, Box 6425, Friday Harbor, WA 98250.

Wallin, Craig. *Backyard Cash Crops: The Source Book for Growing and Marketing Specialty Plants.* Homestead Design Inc., P.O. Box 1058, Bellingham, WA 98227.

Seed Sources

Some companies charge for their catalog. Call first to check prices and availability.

Bountiful Gardens
18001 Shafer Ranch Road
Willits, CA 95490
707/459-6410

Seeds, garden craft items, tools, and supplies, plus beneficial insects.

W. Atlee Burpee & Co.
P.O. Box 5114
Warminster, PA 18974
800/888-1447
www.burpee.com

Seeds only. An all-purpose catalog with a standard selection of seeds at retail prices.

Cook's Garden Seeds
P.O. Box 535
Londonderry, VT 05148
800/457-9703
Fax 800/457-9705
www.cooksgarden.com

Seeds only. Cook's carries nine types of basil, and many annual and perennial herbs.

Foxhill Farm
443 West Michigan Avenue
P.O. Box 9
Parma, MI 49269
517/531-3179
Fax 517/531-3179

Plants year round. They carry a comprehensive selection of scented geraniums, topiaries or espaliers of lavender, rosemary, rose geranium, myrtle, and sweet bay. They also carry many varieties of basil and rosemary.

Johnny's Selected Seeds
1 Foss Hill Road
Albion, ME 04910
207/437-4301
www.johnnyseeds.com

Excellent seeds and very reasonable prices.

Kitazawa Seed Co.
1111 Chapman Street
San Jose, CA 95126
408/243-1330

Seeds for Asian vegetables.

Nichols Garden Nursery
1190 North Pacific Highway
Albany, OR 97321
541/928-9280
www.nicholsgardennursery.com

Seeds and plants. Plants shipped only in spring and fall.

Redwood City Seed Co.
P.O. Box 361
Redwood City, CA 94064
650/325-7333
www.ecoseeds.com

Seeds only. They feature unusual varieties from all over the world. Look for four kinds of cilantro. Specializing in open-pollinated varieties beloved by chefs.

Seeds of Change
1364 Rufina Circle #5
Santa Fe, NM 87501
888/762-7333
www.seedsofchange.com

Organic seeds and many heirloom varieties.

Shepherd's Garden Seeds
30 Irene Street
Torrington, CT 06790
860/482-3638
www.shepherdseeds.com

Seeds and plants. Mail order with a limited selections of herbs, an edible flower collection, and a selection of small plants by mail.

Territorial Seed Co.
P.O. Box 157
Cottage Grove, OR 97424
541/942-9547
www.territorial_seed.com

An extensive list of short-season varieties, plus over 400 varieties of other specialty seeds.

Tomato Growers Supply Co.
P.O. Box 2237
Fort Myers, FL 33902
888/478-7333
www.tomatogrowers.com

Heirloom and hybrid varieties of tomatoes.

Bulb Sources

B. & D. Lilies
284566 Highway 101 S.
Port Townsend, WA 98368
360/765-4341
www.bdlilies.com

Superb selection of lilies with horticultural information.

Daffodil Mart
30 Irene Street
Torrington, CT 06790
800/265-2852
www.800/255-2852

Make sure to use this catalog for its informative text and wide variety of old favorites and newer selection of daffodil bulbs.

Dutch Gardens
P.O. Box 200
Adelphia, NJ 07710
800/818-3861
www.dutchgardens.com

Catalog of standard and newer varieties, with excellent full-page color photographs.

McClure and Zimmerman
108 West Winnebago Street
P.O. Box 368
Friesland, WI 53935
800/883-6998
www.mzbulb.com

Catalogs are mailed in May for fall bulb shipment. Excellent range of standard and unusual bulbs, with original art illustrations and useful horticultural information.

Park Seed
1 Parkton Avenue
Greenwood, SC 29647
800/845-3369
www.parkseed.com

An all-purpose catalog with standard bulbs and a nice array of miniature daffodils.

Peaceful Valley Farm Supply
P.O. Box 2209
Grass Valley, CA 95945
888/784-1722
www.groworganic.com

Wide selection of standard and unusual bulbs, with emphasis on easily grown varieties. Ship only in the fall.

John Sheepers Inc.
P.O. Box 700
Bantam, CT 06750
860/567-0838
Fax 860/567-5323

A catalog of unusual bulb varieties including muscari, scillas, alliums, colchicums, species tulips, and miniature daffodils. Their tulip selection is outstanding.

K. Van Bourgondien & Sons Inc.
P.O. Box 1000
Babylon, NY 11702-0598
800/552-9996
Fax 800/552-9916

This catalog sells large-quantity orders of both standard and unusual bulbs.

Van Engelen Inc.
23 Tulip Drive
Bantam, CT 06750
860/567-8734
www.vanengelen.com
Large-quantity orders of unusual and standard bulbs of all kinds.

Wayside Gardens
Hodges, SC 29695
800/845-1124
www.waysidegardens.com

An all-purpose catalog with a standard mix of bulbs.

White Flower Farm
30 Irene Street
Torrington, CT 06790
800/503-9624
www.whiteflowerfarm.com

A wide selection of varieties of standard bulbs illustrated with color photographs. Lilies, daffodils, and tulips are outstanding.

Professional Associations

American Cheese Society
c/o Laura Jacobs Welch
P.O. Box 303
Delavan, WI 53115
262/728-4458
www.cheesesociety.com

American Farmland Trust
National Office
1200 18th Street N.W., Suite 800
Washington, DC 20036
202/331-7300
800/886-5170
www.farmland.org

American Livestock Breeds Conservancy
P.O. Box 477
Pittsboro, NC 27312
919/542-5704
www.albc_usa.org

An organization working to preserve domestic animals and poultry from extinction. Their excellent newsletter and publications are useful for those raising barnyard exotics.

Animal Finders Guide
c/o Pat Hoctor
P.O. Box 99
Prairie Creek, IN 47869
812/898-2701
www.animalfindersguide.com

Community Alliance with Family Farmers
P.O. Box 363
Davis, CA 95617
530/756-8518

Publishes *Farmer to Farmer, Agrarian Advocate, National Organic Directory,* and *Farm Fresh* a directory of California farmers selling directly to the public from farms to farmers' markets.

North American Deer Farmers Association
9301 Annapolis Road, #206
Lanham, MD 20706
301/459-7708
www.nadefa.org

Small Farm Center
University of California, Davis
Davis, CA 95616
530/752-8136
http://www.sfc.ucdavis.edu

Excellent publications and assistance.

Sources of Printed Materials on Small-Scale Farming

Fertile Ground Book
P.O. Box 2008
Davis, CA 95617
800/540-0170
www.agribooks.com

A good source for books, videotapes,and research services.

Community Alliance with Family Farmers
P.O. Box 464
Davis, CA 95610
800/852-3832 (Publications ordering line)
530/756-8518

Publishers of *National Organic Directory, Farm Fresh Directory* (direct marketing for California farmers), *Farmer to Farmer, and Agrarian Advocate.*

Farming Alternatives Program
Department of Rural Sociology
17 Warren Hall
Cornell University
Ithaca, NY 14853-7801
607/255-9832

Request information on subscribing to their informative and innovative newsletter.

Publications
Agriculture and Natural Resources Communication
    Services
University of California
6701 San Pablo Avenue
Oakland, CA 94608-1239
510/642-2431
800/994-8849
http://anrcatalog.ucdavis.edu

Small Farm Center
University of California, Davis
Davis, CA 95615
530/752-8136
http://www.sfc.ucdavis.edu

A source of written and internet information on crops, poultry, animals, and innovative farm techniques and marketing. Materials on sustainable agriculture are also available in Spanish.

Small Farmer's Journal
P.O. Box 1627
Sisters, OR 97759
541/549-2064

A nuts-and-bolts magazine featuring practical horse farming.

USDA Cooperative State Research, Education and
    Extension Service
Small Farm Program
1400 Independence Avenue SW
Stop 2220
Washington, DC 20050
202/401-6544
http://www.reeusda.gov/smallfarm

They offer a variety of useful pamphlets on every subject from cashmere goats to cut flowers for sale and profit. Request the free, informative, and lively quarterly newsletter.

INDEX

A

Acorns, 43
Adams, Patti, 34
Adams Station Produce, 34, 90
Advertising, 82–83, 110, 154, 160. *See also* Publicity
for herb products, 167
for specialty potatoes, 151–152
for U-pick operations, 92–93, 146
Agricultural adviser, 2, 140
farm agent, 176, 177, 180, 183
for organic certification, 13, 21, 139
for specialty crop selection, 33
Agricultural literacy, 101, 107
Agriculture, regional, 2–3
Agritourism, 146, 158, 161, 164
farm trail organizations, 93
as rural industry, 102
Alar (pesticide), 15, 18, 19
Almonds, 52
Amish community
farm festivals, 110–111
as small-farm model, 27
Anderson, Graham, 60
Animals. *See also* specific animals
advantages/disadvantages of, 179, 181, 188
cover crops for, 15
in diversified production, 27–28, 172, 179, 180–181, 184–185, 186–187

for fertilizer production, 14, 21, 28, 47, 172, 178, 179, 180, 184
for meat production, 60–61
nonfood products from, 61, 172
organic certification for, 13, 21
precautions of, 182, 183, 185
for urban farm, 128
Antiques, 54
Antique varieties. *See* Heirloom varieties
Apple Barn, The, 156–159
Apples, 3, 6, 49, 121–122
Granny Smith, 32
Homestead Orchards, 160–163
pesticide use on, 15–16
Pettigrew Fruit Orchard, 153–155
as specialty crop, 32

B

Baby vegetables, as specialty crop, 29, 31
Bagley, Lynn, 85
Bar codes, 67–68, 143
Barter, for materials exchange, 47, 126, 176
Basalt dust, 14
Basil, 31, 39, 124
Bay (California Laurel), 60
Bed and breakfast inn, 1, 103–106
Beekeeping, 47, 54
in cities, 126–127
Bees, plants attracting, 35

Ben and Jerry's ice cream, 69
Berries, 43, 44, 54. *See also*
    specific kinds
    as forage crop, 49–50
Binsberger, Jim, 160–163
Biological agriculture. *See*
    Sustainable agriculture
Biological controls, replacing
    pesticide use, 16, 17
Birds, exotic, 128, 184, 185
Bitter melons, 31
Black Kettle Farm, 144–147
Blood meal, 14
Blueberries, 5
Blueberry preserves, 61
Bone meal, 14
Breed Associations
    American Minor Breeds, 14,
    189
Broccoli, 59
Brokers. *See also* Wholesalers
    for herbs, 38
    for value-added products,
    64
Bulbs, 123
Burls, 44, 54

C

California Vegetable
    Specialties, 96
Candles, 43, 45, 127
Canter-Berry Farms, 61, 180
Caplan, Frieda, 33
Cash flow. *See also* Marketing
    plan
    analyzing in marketing
    plan, 62–63
    diversified crops providing,
    76
    establishing goals for, 78
Catalog, for mail order, 95,
    152
Cattails, 43

Cattle 176, 179, 181, 182,
    187–189
Cedar, deodar, 49
Celeriac, 29
Celestial Seasonings, 38, 69
Chadwick, Alan, 25
Cheese, 61, 188
Chefs. *See* Cooking;
    Restaurants
Chemicals. *See* Fertilizer;
    Herbicides; Pesticides
Cherries, 49, 121. *See also*
    Fruit trees
Chickens, 7, 8, 128, 146, 179,
    180, 181, 184, 185. *See*
    also Animals
Child, Julia, 4
Children
    farm education programs
    for, 114–115, 146, 161
    farm festivals for, 110–112,
    113
    pesticide residues affecting,
    15, 16
    wholesome food for, 20, 101
Chili, 31, 57–58, 125
Chinese vegetables, 31
Chives, 123
Christmas trees, 60
Cider, 157, 159
Cilantro, 32, 124
City gardens. *See* Urban
    farming
City Worms and Compost,
    168–170
Clover, 14. *See also* Cover
    crops
Coil, Dorothy, 80
Coleman, Eliot, 25
Collins, Rich, 96
Colusa Cold Storage, 80
Commodities, distinct from
    specialty crops, 30–32
Commodity boards, 137–138
Community sustained

agriculture, 112–114, 129, 165
Companion planting. *See* Intercropping
Compost. *See also* Fertilizer; Recycling
City Worms and Compost, 168–170
for soil fertility, 14
Conserve, 59
Container gardening, 30, 119. *See also* Planter baskets; Raised beds; Urban farming
Container plants
Christmas trees, 60
planter baskets, 60, 124, 125
Contracts, for picnic facility use, 107–108
Cooking. *See also* Kitchens; Restaurants
for bed and breakfast inns, 103, 105
with herbs, 36
regulation kitchens for, 64
for value-added products, 59
Co-packagers, 71–72
Corn
Golden Jubilee, 34
in intercropping, 30
miniature, 31
Costs
analyzing for value-added products, 64–65, 72–73
customer education about, 162
farm expenses, 172
of organic certification, 22
Cotton, 23
County extension agents, 140
County health department, 141–142
Cover crops
in diversified production, 28

in organic farming, 14–15, 16, 17, 21, 151
scavenging for profit, 43
in sustainable agriculture, 13
Coyote Cookhouse Salsa, 69
Crab apples, 49
Crop rotation
in diversified production, 28
in sustainable agriculture, 13, 17
Cross, Doug, 61
CSA. *See* Community sustained agriculture
Cucumbers, 30
Culinary Institute of America, 167
Customers
agricultural literacy for, 101
educating, 85–86, 112, 152, 155, 161–162, 163
at farmers' markets, 84, 85
farm festivals for, 110–113, 161, 166
mail-order, 94–96
neighbors as, 128–129
relationship with, 76–77, 79–82, 150
specialty crops for, 34
urban, 42–43, 101–102, 129–130

D

D&M Gardens, 26
Daffodils, 52, 76
Daikon, 29, 31
Daminozide, 15
Deforestation, 16
Delmont, Stephanie, 26
Dependability, 81
Desertification, 16
Dill, 29, 36
Direct sales. *See* Mail-order;

U-pick operations
Distributors. *See*
    Wholesalers
Diversification of crops
    in farmers' markets, 87
    for maximizing profit, 27–
        28, 76–77
    necessity for, 8
    in organic farming, 17
    for U-pick operations, 88
Dogs, 181
Drip systems, 26
Dubit, Wendy, 115
Ducks, 104, 146, 184, 185
    products from, 8–9, 128

E

Eating in France (Wells), 102
Ecological Farming
    Conference, 23
Education. *See also* Publicity
    about compost and worms,
        169
    for farm customers, 85–86,
        112, 152, 155, 161–162,
        163
Eggplant, 26, 31
Eggs, 7, 9, 76
    duck, 128
    quail, 128
    specialty, 61
E-mail. *See* Internet
Employees, 81–82. *See also*
    Labor costs
    federal regulations for, 136
    safety training for, 133
    for U-pick operations, 88,
        89
Entrepreneurial spirit, 8, 9
Equipment
    benefits of new and used,
        173, 174, 177, 178
    expenses of, 173, 174

renting, 176
Ethnic cuisine, 31, 121
Eucalyptus trees, 51
European specialties, 5

F

Faison, David, 48–49
Family farms, 5, 6–7
Farm adviser. *See*
    Agricultural adviser
Farmer Brown's Farm, 110
    111, 115
Farmers' markets. *See also*
    Community sustained
    agriculture; U-pick
    operations
    booth design for, 86–87
    city and suburban, 1, 5–6, 78
    in France, 101–102
    kitchens for, 142
    maximizing returns from,
        83–87
    regulations affecting, 84,
        142
    supporting organic produce,
        19
Farm Hands-City Hands, 114
Farming. *See also* Container
    gardening; Market
    gardening; Organic
    farming; Sustainable
    agriculture; Urban
    farming
    bees for pollination, 127
    business practices for, 7, 9
    conventional, 2, 16, 27
    equipment costs, 2
    marketing advice for, 46
    systems, 171–172, 173, 180
Farm inspections, 2
Farm stores, for retail sales,
    145–147
Farm trail organizations, 93.

See also Agritourism
Fast food, 3
Fava beans, 14
FDA (Food and Drug Admin-
    istration) requirements,
    67, 68
Fences, 30
Fertilizer. *See also* Compost;
    Cover crops; Manure
    animals providing, 2, 7, 8,
        14, 21, 28, 47
    organic, 12, 14, 21
    synthetic, 17
Festivals, 110–112, 164. *See
    also* Agritourism
Fiddleneck fern, 50, 152
Fig leaves, 123
Findlay Market, 5
Firewood, 55
Fishermen, farm products for,
    8
Fish ponds, 132–133
Flavor. *See also* Quality
    of commercial fruit, 3
    educating customers about,
        86
    harvesting procedures
        enhancing, 33
    organic methods enhancing,
        19
    in small-farm produce, 5
    in value-added products,
        59
Fleece, 61, 165, 188
Florists, providing materials
    for, 43–46, 52, 55, 122
Flower markets, 46
Flowers bulbs, 123
    cut, 122–123
    dried, 43, 52, 55, 76, 123
    edible, 122
    foraged, 52
Food columnists, 82–83
Foraging, 8, 42–56

for herbs, 166
marketing procedures for,
    44–46, 76
on public land, 53–54
of wild/naturalized plants,
    49–52
4-H program, 111, 115
Foxes, 185
Fraises du bois, 101
France
    farmers' markets in,
        101–102
    herb sales in, 35, 124
French intensive method, 25–
    27
Freshness, 3–4, 6
    FDA requirements for, 67
    ripeness, 154
    in value-added products, 9
Frieda's Finest Produce
    Specialties, 33
Fruit, 3, 9
    pesticide use on, 16–17
    timely delivery for, 74–75
Fruit leather, 126
Fruit trees, 7, 8, 119
    bartering for care of, 120
    dwarf, 89, 120
    for floral branches, 51, 52
    as long-term investment, 49
    naturalizing, 51
    on Pettigrew Fruit Orchard,
        153–155
    recycling prunings from, 8,
        42, 43, 55, 159
    recycling wood from, 48–49
    for U-pick operations,
        89–90
    for value-added products,
        57–58
Fujimoto, Bill, 154
Full Belly Farm, 111, 164–166
Fungicides, 22. *See also*
    Organic farming; Pesticides

G

Gardens. *See also* Container
    gardening; Market
    gardening
  classes about, 130–131
  installing for profit,
    129–130
  intercropping chart for,
    28–29
Garlic, 35–36, 59, 123–124
Garlic braids, 125
Geese, 104, 180, 181, 184
Gerbers, 7
Ginseng, 35, 50–51, 55
Gizdich Farm, 32, 89, 111–112
Goats, 47, 61, 104, 181, 182,
    187–189
Gourds, 160, 166
Gourmet Retailer, 20
Grasses, dried, 44, 55
Greenbelts, 7
Green Markets, 5
Greens (floral), 44, 55, 76, 125
Green Terrestrial, 166–168
Growing season, 28–29, 36
Guano products, 14

H

Haricots verts, 31
Harvest. *See also* U-pick
    operations; Value-added
    products
  extending with varieties,
    28–29
  organic postharvest
    handling, 21–22
  procedures for, 33
Harvester, The, 50
Haywagon rides, 111
Hedgerows, 13
Heirloom varieties, restoration
    of, 5

Herbicides. *See also* Organic
    farming; Pesticides
  health risks of, 15–17
  in organic farming, 12–13,
    17
Hens, 184
Herbs, 1, 7, 30, 119. *See also*
    specific kinds
  Asian, 121
  culinary, 36
  as foraged crop, 50–51, 52,
    55
  fresh, 123–124
  Green Terrestrial farm, 166–
    168
  in intercropping, 29
  marketing procedures for,
    38–39, 77
  medicinal, 36–38, 77, 166–
    167
  raised beds for, 26
  as specialty crop, 31, 34–36
  for tea, 38–39, 166
  Well-Sweep Farm, 163–164
Holmes, Chris, 150–152
Homestead Orchards,
    160–163
Honey, 126–127. *See also*
    Beekeeping
Horses, 8, 111, 180
Hummingbirds, 35
Hussey, Barbara, 103
Hybrid varieties, 5
Hyde, Louise, 163–164

I

Inputs, 14, 27
Insects beneficial
  cover crops enhancing, 13,
    15
  resistance to pesticides, 16
Insurance, 2, 109. *See also*
    Regulations

for bed and breakfast
operation, 105
for farm activities, 133
for product liability, 142–
143
for U-pick operations,
89–90
for value-added products, 65
Integrated pest management,
11, 12
for apple orchard, 153
cover crop use in, 15
in sustainable agriculture,
13
Intensive gardening methods, 7
French, 25–27
Intercropping, 29
Internet
addresses, 193
costs, 192
finding the right service,
192
learning to use, 191
obtaining information, 192,
193
researching on, 193
setting up Web page, 194
sites, 194–195
sources, 189
IPM. *See* Integrated pest
management
Iron Kettle Farm, 144–147
Irrigation drip systems, 26
USDA advice for, 135–136
Island Sun Greenhouses, 60

J

Jackson, Jeanne, 144–147
Jams, 57, 61, 126
Jansen, Burtis, 80
Jeavons, John, 25
Jellies, 57, 126

Jerusalem artichoke, 50

K

Kilpatrick, Bill, 156–159
Kitchens. *See also* Cooking
for bed and breakfast inns,
103
for farmers' markets, 142
health department codes
for, 141
for value-added products,
64, 132
Kona Kai Gardens, 26
Kraus, Sibella, 4

L

Labels
bar codes for, 67–68
designing, 68–70
federal regulations affecting,
136
for organic growers, 22
for value-added products,
66–67
Labor costs, 2, 64–65. *See
also* Employees
Land
bartering for use of, 119
cost of, 2
leasing, 120
organic certification for, 13
public, foraging on, 53–54
Legumes, 15
Lemon verbena, 52
Lettuce, 3, 4, 119, 122, 124
fertility requirements, 12
in intercropping, 29, 30
raised beds for, 26–27
as urban cash crop, 26
Loggers, 1

M

McCrumm, Tom, 147–150
McDonald's, 3
McFadden Farms, 59–60
McFadden, Guinness, 59–60
McGuigan, Richard, 66
Mail-order
    advantages/disadvantages,
        94–96
    for herb products, 164, 167
    for maple sugar farm, 149–
        150
    for orchard products, 158,
        160–161
Manure, 8, 14, 47, 76. *See
    also* Fertilizer
Maple syrup, 47–48, 55, 147–
    150
Marin Farmers' Market, 85
Marjoram, 125
Market gardening, 4–5, 7, 12.
    See also Specialty crops;
        Urban farming
Marketing orders, 137
Marketing plan. *See also*
    Research; Selling
    for apple orchard, 160
    for cash-flow analysis, 62–
        63, 76, 78
    components of, 75–76
    for diversified crop, 9
    for niche marketing, 39–40,
        162
    for value-added products,
        9, 61–64
MeadowView Country
    Gardens, 103
Meat production, 9, 60–61.
    See also Animals
Medicine, 36–38, 50. *See also*
    Herbs
Melons, 30, 40

Milk, 61
Minerals, 14
Mint, 30, 31, 52, 124
Mistletoe, 44, 53, 55
Monckton, Lisa, 129
Money-saving tactics 173–174
Monterey Market, 154
Montgomery, Pam, 166–168
Moss, 53, 55
Mushrooms, 50, 55

N

Narcissus, 52
Nasturtiums, 123, 124
National Forests, 42, 53
National Institutes of Health,
    37
Natural Resources Defense
    Council, 15
Neighbors,
    advantages of, 174, 176
    as customers, 128–129
    hiring, 176
Nelson, Cindy, 168–170
Newman's Own, 7
New Penny Farm, 150–152
Niche marketing, 39–40, 162
Nicotine spray, 21
Nigella, 52
Nitrogen. *See also* Fertilizer
    cover crops producing, 15,
        16, 21, 28
    in synthetic fertilizer, 17
Northwest Botanical, 53
Norton, Michael, 26
Nursery starts, 60
    for U-pick operations, 88
    as urban crop, 124–125
Nutrition Labeling and
    Education Act, 136
Nuts, 44

O

Oats, 14
Oranges, 121, 122
Orchards, 57–58. *See also*
    Fruit trees
Oregano, 125
Organic Farmer, 18, 23
Organic farming, 11, 24
  certification procedures,
      12–13, 20–21, 84, 132,
      138–139
  for community sustained
      agriculture, 113
  criteria for, 12
  Full Belly Farm, 111, 164–
      166
  for herbs, 123, 163
  organizations for, 23
  for potatoes, 150–152
  profitability for, 19–20
  quality concerns for, 18–19
  research funds for, 116
  vs. sustainable farming,
      17–18
Organic Foods Protection
    Act, 11–12, 20, 22, 138
Organic produce
  advantages/disadvantages,
      7–8
  profitability of, 19–20
Ostrich, 61

P

Packaging for foraged
    materials, 45
  for fruit, 154
  for value-added products,
      61, 62, 63
Paperwork, 22, 160. *See also*
    Regulations
Peaches, 57, 160
Pears, 153–155

Peas, 97
Pea tendrils, 31, 121
Permits. *See* Regulations
Persimmons, 43–44
Pesticides. *See also*
    Herbicides; Organic
    farming
  biological controls
      replacing, 16, 17
  health risks of, 15–17
  in integrated pest
      management, 13
  in organic farming, 7, 12, 17,
      21, 22
  public response to, 15–16
  USDA regulations for, 134–
      135
Pests, 30
Peters, Ellis, 37
Pettigrew Fruit, 153–155
Petting zoo, 88, 102, 115, 161,
    189
Photographs, for advertising,
    107
Picnic facilities, 106–109
Pigs, 8, 179, 180
Pike Street Market, 5
Pine cones, 43, 44, 53, 55, 126
Pine needles, 8, 53
Pippin Ridge Orchard, 62
Planning department, 141
Planter baskets. *See also*
    Container gardening
  for edible plants, 124–125
  as value-added product, 60
Planting charts, 28–29
Planting records, 30
Plums, 49, 123. *See also* Fruit
    trees
Pollution, 11
Ponds, 132–133
Popcorn, Faith, 46
Porter, Gene Stratton, 50
Potatoes, 3, 7, 150–152
Potpourri, 8, 43, 45, 55

Prices, 9
Produce. *See also* Fruit;
    Organic farming;
    Vegetables
  commercial requirements
    for, 2–3
  quality concerns for, 18–19
Produce baskets, 128–129
Profitability of Amish farms, 27
  of foraged goods, 45, 46
Publicity, 9, 82–83. *See also*
    Advertising
  for bed and breakfast
    operation, 106
  for maple sugar farm, 148–149
  for U-pick operation, 92–93
Pumpkins, 110–111, 129, 160,
    162–163
  for U-pick operations,
    145–146
Pyrethrum, 21

Q

Quail eggs, 128, 184
Quality. *See also* Flavor
  commodity boards main-
    taining, 137
  customer insistence for, 152
  superseding quantity, 40
  wholesalers advice for, 154
Quince trees, 52. *See also*
    Fruit trees

R

Rabbits, 111, 128, 179, 186–
    187. *See also* Animals
Raccoons, 185
Radish, 29
Raised beds, 12, 25–26, 119.
    See also Container
    gardening

Realtors, 123
Recipes
  providing with products,
    83, 86
  for value-added products,
    59
Recycling for increased profit,
    42, 76
  for increasing soil fertility,
    17
  for reducing inputs, 14, 27
  of retail supplies, 60
Redwood Hill Goat Dairy, 47
Regional agriculture, 2–3, 5
Regulations
  affecting organic farms, 7,
    11–13, 20–22
  affecting water use, 139
  analyzing in marketing
    plan, 62
  for bed and breakfast inns,
    103–104
  for farm activity, 2, 132–133
  for farmers' markets, 84,
    142
  for farm fishpond, 133
  for foraging, 53–54
  for labels, 66–69, 136
  for medicinal herbs, 37
  for name registration,
    68–69
  for nursery sales, 124
  for organic farms, 11–12
  for pesticides, 134–135
  for U-pick operations, 89
  USDA requirements, 134–
    136
  for value-added products,
    9, 64–65, 124
Rent Mother Nature, 48
Research. *See also* Marketing
    plan
  for culinary herbs, 36
  for farmers' markets, 84
  for foraged products, 44–46

for increasing sales, 77–78

Research, *continued*
for market garden, 120–122
on farm research, 115–116
for value-added products,
58–61

Restaurants
for on-farm income, 48,
157–158, 159
organic produce
requirements, 7–8, 19
pros/cons of selling to, 96–
98
specialty crops for, 31, 77,
153–154
stimulating demand for
quality produce, 4

Ripeness, 154. *See also*
Freshness; Quality

Rivers, Dru, 164–166

Roadside stands, 5–6, 145.
See also U-pick operations

Rock phosphate, 14

Roosters, 8, 128

Rosehips, 42, 55

Rosemary, 36, 52, 163

Roses, 47, 51, 55, 108–109

Rushes, 43

Rye, 14

S

Sachets, 45

Safety education, 133

Salmonberries, 49

Scavenging, 42. *See also*
Foraging; Recycling

School programs, 114–115,
189

Seasonal eating, 5

Seedpods, 43, 44, 122

Seeds, 36, 52

Selling, 7, 9, 74–100, 155. *See
also* Marketing plan

foraged goods, 45–46
labels for, 66–67, 68–70

Shallots, 36

Sheep, 6, 8, 179, 180, 181,
182, 187–189

Sherrill, Donna, 74

Signs, 93–94, 138

Skiing, 102, 103

Skins, 61

Skunks, 185

Small, Sally, 153–155

Soil. *See also* Compost; Cover
crops; Fertilizer
determining crops for, 33
fertility, 14, 16–17, 28, 151
in organic farming, 12, 14,
166

Soil conservation service,
135–136

Sonka, Evelyn, 105

Sonka's Sheep Station, 105

South Face Farm, 147–150

Soybeans, 14

Specialty crops
baby vegetables, 29, 31
in community sustained
agriculture, 114
defining, 30–31
exotic, 31–32
intensive methods for,
25–30
lettuce, 12
niche marketing for, 39–40
potatoes, 150–152
selecting, 32–33, 34, 121
for U-pick operations, 88
vegetables and herbs, 25–41

Specialty products, 9–10

Specialty stores
produce tasting at, 83
supporting quality produce,
4, 19–20

Spices, 31. *See also* Herbs

Squash, 31, 40, 80, 85, 129

Strawberries, 145

Subscription farming, 112–114, 129, 165
Succession cropping, 25–27
Summer savory, 36
Sunflowers, 30, 50, 111
Supermarkets, 20
Sustainable agriculture. *See also* Organic farming
  community involvement with, 112–114
  techniques for, 13, 18
  vs. organic farming, 17–18
Swags, 125–126

T

Tarragon, 36
Taste. *See* Flavor
Taxes, 2, 104, 140, 159
Tea, herbal, 38–39
Texture, 3, 5
Thimbleberries, 49
Thyme, 36, 163
Tingle, Alta, 46
Tomatillos, 31–32
Tomatoes, 3, 8, 19, 84, 90, 97, 119
  cherry, 124
  Green Grape, 121
  in intercropping, 29
  as specialty crop, 121
  succession planting for, 29–30
  Tigerella, 34
  trellises for, 30
  for U-pick operations, 145
Tours, for farm visits, 93, 102, 146, 158, 161, 164, 189
Traditional Medicinals, 38
Trains, 2–3
Transportation, 2–3
Trees
  Christmas, 60
  for lumber, 48–49, 51

Trellises, 30
Tulips, 52, 110
Turnips, 29

U

Universal product codes, 67–68, 143
U-pick operations. *See also* Farmers' markets
  advantages/disadvantages, 87–94
  crops for, 145
  customer amenities for, 91–92
  insurance for, 89–90
  picnic facilities for, 106–109
  regulations affecting, 89
Urban customers agricultural literacy for, 101–102
  agritourism for, 102
  garden planning service for, 129–130
  products for, 42–43
Urban farming, 25, 119–131. *See also* Container gardening
  containers for, 30
  lettuce growing, 1
USDA (U.S. Department of Agriculture) regulations, 134–135

V

Value-added products, 9, 28, 57–73
  bar codes for, 67–68, 143
  chili, 32
  co-packagers for, 71–72
  defined, 58
  herbs, 36, 124, 164
  for maple sugar farm, 150

Value-added products,
    continued
  marketing plan for, 61–64
  market research for, 58–61
  nonfood products, 59–61
  pricing strategy for, 72–73
  supplies for, 70–71
  for U-pick operations, 88
Varietal forms, 3, 29
Vegetables, 3, 9, 17
  baby, 29, 31
  Chinese, 31
  commercial requirements
    for, 3
  specialty, 25–41
  in value-added products, 9
  varieties and harvesting
    dates, 29–30
Vinegar, 52, 66–67, 124, 164

W

Wade, Isabelle, 47
Walnuts, 59
Watermelons, 12, 17, 33
Waters, Alice, 4
Water use, regulations
    affecting, 139
Webster, Anne, 122
Weeds
  animals for reducing, 28,
    128
  chemical control for, 18
  cover crops for controlling,
    15
  organic control for, 17
Weed, Susan, 167
Weights and measures, 142

Wells, Patricia, 102
Well-Sweep Farm, 163–164
Wholesalers, 4, 9, 152. *See
    also* Brokers
  advantages/disadvantages
    of, 98–99
  difficulties with, 74–75
  requiring organic produce,
    19
  for selling foraged goods, 46
  for value-added supplies,
    59
Willows, 43
Wisteria, 122
Wonnacott, Enid, 18
Wooden Shoe Bulb Company,
    110
Woodlots, 51. *See also* Trees
Wool, 61
World Wide Web. *See* Internet
Worms, 16, 168–170
Wreaths, 6, 43–45, 55, 59–60,
    95, 123, 125–126, 164,
    166. *See also* Value-
    added products

Y

Yarrow, 52

Z

Zoning
  affecting farm use, 140–141,
    159
  for bed and breakfast
    operation, 104

Turn Your Dream into Reality

Millions of people just like you are enjoying the freedom—and extra income—of working for themselves. You can too. It's incredibly easy to start a money-making business right from the comfort of your own home. In this book, home-based business guru Ty Hicks shows you how to achieve your work-at-home dream. Inside you'll learn the secrets to:

- **Choosing the home-based business that's just right for you**

- **Getting started in your business with minimal cost**

- **Building your fortune doing what you love**

- **Running a business from home while keeping your day job**

- **Using the Internet to advertise and promote your home-based business**

- **And much more!**

ISBN 0-7615-1743-X
Paperback / 288 pages
U.S. $14.95 / Can. $22.00

**To order, call (800) 632-8676 or
visit us online at www.primalifestyles.com**

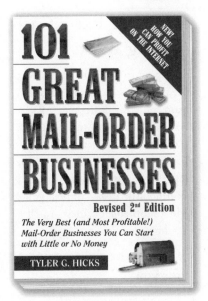

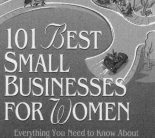

To Order Books

Please send me the following items:

Quantity	Title	Unit Price	Total
_____	**101 Best Small Businesses for Women**	$ _____	$ _____
_____	**101 Great Mail-Order Businesses**	$ _____	$ _____
_____	**199 Great Home Businesses You Can Start (and Succeed In) for Under $1000, Revised 2nd Edition**	$ _____	$ _____
_____	**How to Start Your Own Business on a Shoestring and Make Up to $500,000 a Year**	$ _____	$ _____

Subtotal	$ _____
7.25% Sales Tax (CA only)	$ _____
7% Sales Tax (PA only)	$ _____
5% Sales Tax (IN only)	$ _____
7% G.S.T. Tax (Canada only)	$ _____
Priority Shipping	$ _____
Total Order	$ _____

FREE
Ground Freight
in U.S. and Canada

Foreign and all Priority Request orders:
Call Customer Service
for price quote at 916-787-7000

By Telephone: With American Express, MC, or Visa,
call 800-632-8676, Monday–Friday, 8:30–4:30.
www.primapublishing.com
By E-mail: sales@primapub.com
By Mail: Just fill out the information below
and send with your remittance to:
Prima Publishing ▪ P.O. Box 1260BK ▪ Rocklin, CA 95677

Name _____

Address _____

City _____ State _____ ZIP_____

American Express/MC/Visa# _____ Exp. _____

Check/money order enclosed for $_____ Payable to Prima Publishing

Daytime telephone _____

Signature _____